Become an Ironman
An Amateur's Guide to Participating in the World's Toughest Endurance Event

Portions of this book first appeared in the author's column on www.biobuilde.com.

A version of Part VII was originally written by the author for the book *Triathlon for Women: A Mind-Body-Spirit Approach for Female Athletes*, by Lisa Lynam (Meyer & Meyer, 2006) and is reprinted here with her kind permission.

Ironman Edition

BECOME AN IRONMAN
An Amateur's Guide to Participating in the World's Toughest Endurance Event

by Cherie Gruenfeld

Meyer & Meyer Sport

IRONMAN® is a registered trademark of World Triathlon Corporation

British Library Cataloguing in Publication Data
A catalogue record for this book is available from the British Library

Cherie Gruenfeld, Become an Ironman
Maidenhead: Meyer & Meyer Sport (UK) Ltd., 2008
ISBN 978-1-84126-113-3

© 2008 by Meyer & Meyer Sport (UK) Ltd.
Aachen, Adelaide, Auckland, Budapest, Graz, Indianpolis, Johannesburg,
Maidenhead, New York, Olten (CH), Singapore, Toronto
Member of the World
Sport Publishers' Association (WSPA)
www.w-s-p-a.org
Printed and bound by: B.O.S.S Druck und Medien GmbH, Germany
ISBN 978-1-84126-113-3
E-Mail: verlag@m-m-sports.com
www.m-m-sports.com

Contents

Photo & Illustration Credits

Cover Photo:	Cherie & Lee Gruenfeld
Cover Design:	Jens Vogelsang
Inside Photos:	see captions

INTRODUCTION

Why?

I'm 63 years old. Madison Avenue marketing types will have you believe that "60 is the new 50" and that may be. But any way you look at it, there's no denying that I have more years of living behind me than ahead. Many folks my age are taking this time to reflect on past accomplishments while relaxing and enjoying a well-earned rest. A swimming pool is for drinking mai tais while floating on a plastic raft, a bike is transportation to the local cafe for Sunday morning brunch, and running? That's something better left to the young kids.

But that's not this 63-year-old. I just finished writing my goals for next year and, in order to accomplish them, I'm going to have to rise at 5:00 a.m. to swim lap after lap in the pool, cover mega-miles on solo bike rides where my only destination is right back where I started, and as for running...I'm going to have to use some of the energy of the young kids I train with to help me run faster. I'm not ready to look back and concede that it's been a great ride. I still have goals to meet and big moments ahead.

You might ask why. Why am I still driven to challenge myself with such hard goals? Why do I find happiness in something that is anything but relaxing?

The answer lies in a little piece of serendipity that touched my life 15 years ago. It's called Ironman. My first one changed my life in more ways than I could possibly have imagined. And in the years since then I've done 17 more of them and it just keeps getting better.

My intent in writing this book was to encourage others to take this life-altering journey and, having done so once, to do it again and again, because each time is different and each time is special. I've struggled for a means of describing why Ironman is such a remarkable experience, the emotions it evokes in me and why I speak of it as "life-altering." I believe that perhaps the best way to do that is to ask you to step back with me and share my very first Ironman experience, which just happened to be at the World Championships in Kailua-Kona, Hawai'i. But if your first is Lake Placid, Canada, Germany, New Zealand or any other venue, it's your Ironman and, I promise you, the effect on you will be much the same.

October, 1992

My husband Lee and I are on a plane, surrounded by rollicking vacationers imbibing very early in the day. The plane is going to the Hawaiian islands and these folks are going to have a good time.

I, on the other hand, am about to throw up.

I've been scared since the day in August when I unexpectedly qualified for Kona at Mike & Rob's Most Excellent Triathlon and my level of anxiety is rising with every passing mile. It doesn't get any better after we land. Pre-race days in Kona are a wild roller-coaster ride. Some moments I feel high, knowing that I'm trained and believe that I can handle this monster of a challenge. Other times I find myself slipping, riding a downward wave of insecurity. But, there's no stopping time. This is no longer a mental exercise. Race day is about to happen and, this year, I'm going to be part of the action.

Race Day, 6:55 a.m.

The worst part of an Ironman day isn't the pain that happens when you sit on a bike for 112 miles or the struggle to put one foot in front of the other in the closing miles of the run. The worst part of an Ironman day is right now, treading water with 1,400 other crazed athletes pumped up to near hysteria on a mixture of adrenaline and fear. There's a lot of sound but it's unintelligible, just one big chaotic noise: media helicopters overhead, the announcer's microphone blaring instructions you can't make out, lifeguards on surfboards yelling at us to stay behind the line, racers yelling at friends as they spot each other....

And suddenly, without warning...BOOM! The cannon starts the 1992 Ironman. Arms are flailing, feet are kicking and it seems no one is finding water, just other bodies. A smack in the head, my hand catches someone's arm but it's all just part of an Ironman swim. 1,400 swimmers in a small area may look great in those famous photos, but for those of us actually in the water it's like anything-goes wrestling in a washing machine.

The swimmers eventually spread out a little, but for pretty much the entire 2.4 miles, there is contact — some of it not so gentle — until we reach the exit ramp that puts us back on the pier.

This is where I get my first taste of that legendary Ironman support, the cheering for each and every swimmer as we exit and what seems like thousands of volunteers in attendance: in the tents, helping us change and offering encouragement; handing us food and drink;

slathering SPF on our shoulders as we run to the racks; getting even the most disoriented athlete to the right place; pulling our bikes out and handing them to us; reminding us to be careful in the crowded stretch getting out of transition. All of this is so vital and so appreciated that I take a few seconds to thank them.

The course immediately takes us up a big hill before turning onto the highway for the long trek to the turn-around. Raucous crowds line the single lane and their screaming and clapping creates an energy that feels like it's pushing me from behind. It's the best tailwind I've ever had. Because I'm a first-timer here, I don't realize that this is the last I'm going to see of any good-sized crowds until the turnaround in Hawi.

On the bike I encounter every condition possible; winds, heat, humidity and even a couple of rain showers. I run the whole gamut of emotions during the 112 miles; thrill at being there, negative thoughts in the bad patches, feeling like Lance during the good patches, and a few moments of questioning my sanity. At mile 20 I think it's too easy and at mile 80 I think it's too long. At mile 112 I think, "I need to get off this bike."

T2 comes as welcome relief. At this point, I'm so happy to be done with the bike I'm not even thinking about the daunting 26.2 miles ahead. Again, the volunteers seem to be everywhere and this time their goal is to make sure we get out on the run, because there's some food and drink in the changing tent and chairs to sit in and right now it sure seems like a place I'd like to stay for awhile. But I have a job to do and there's a loopy grin plastered on my face because I'm actually doing Ironman! Who would have thought?

So out I go onto the marathon course.

My prior athletic experience had been as a marathoner, so I feel very much under control now. I've never run a marathon after a 2.4 mile swim and a 112 mile bike ride, but at least I'm warmed up. Things are going well and I have a couple of very high moments when I see Lee and my family and when I pass a couple of competitors in my age group. In both instances, I stand a little taller and run with a lighter step. Doesn't last long, but it feels good while it does. I fight a brief low when I turn off Ali'i Drive and head up the hill to the highway. The helicopters are hovering overhead and the crowds are going wild. I'd like to think it's for me, but no such luck. It's for the women's leader who will be at the finish line in one mile. This causes one of those bad patches, thinking that in a few minutes she gets the pleasure of the finish line while I have another 15 miles to go.

Along the highway I see those young, fast kids heading towards me, on their way home. I high-five a few friends and secretly wish I could turn around and run back with them. Ahead I see the Natural Energy Lab where we'll turn and do a little out-and-back. Where I come from that's called "make work." It's necessary mileage to make the 26.2 mile distance, but there is some good associated with it. As I'm running that piece, the sun begins to set. Swaying palm trees are silhouetted against a bright red sky and the sun is gigantic and shimmering like liquid as it drops toward the water. Across this setting a jet, dark against the brilliant backdrop, slides out across the ocean. In a different universe, I'd enjoy this view sipping a nice cabernet. But tonight, there is business at hand and I have six miles to cover before the goal is accomplished.

Five of those six miles put me in a world unlike any I've ever experienced. I am surrounded by pitch black nothingness. The only sound is my own labored breathing and the slapping of my feet as they touch the ground. It's total sensory deprivation. The thought crosses my mind: if I collapsed on the road right now, how long would it be before anyone discovered me? Strange how your mind works in this kind of emptiness.

It's been said that folks who do Ironman suffer through the first 140 miles just so that they can experience that last 0.6. It's true and I was about to get the payback for those first 140. My life is about to change, and in those last seconds of dark and quiet, for the first time all day I allow myself to think about the enormity of the journey I've been on. Months ago I'd set a goal and this morning I'd put it all on the line, attempting the toughest physical challenge of my life. During the day I found that I could stand up to my demons and go farther, suffer more pain and push myself harder than I ever thought possible. And now I was coming home a different person than when I began.

I turn the corner and start the last half mile. The crowds lining the road see me coming and start to clap and yell. The closer I get, the larger and louder the crowd becomes, again providing that tailwind I felt on the hill so many hours ago. As I get closer to the finish line, the lights are so bright I can no longer make out individual spectators, but the noise keeps growing louder and stronger. Soon I'm in the fenced area of the road and high-fiving spectators holding out their hands. No Olympic champion has ever felt better than I'm feeling right now. My tired legs are a thing of the past and I'm sprinting, or at least what passes for sprinting at this point. That makes the crowd even more frenzied, which makes me run faster. With one step left I hear Mike "Voice of Ironman" Reilly booming out over the loudspeakers: "Cherie Gruenfeld....You. Are. An. *Ironman*!"

Could it be? Is it possible? After all these months of saying "I'm going to do an Ironman," have I really done it? My husband, my family and all those thousands of cheering spectators tell me I have.

When I left this very place this morning, I knew I would return, but what I didn't know was what I would learn in the interim. Now I do. I understand something about myself that I didn't know before, about what I'm made of deep inside. I know that I've done something that only a relatively small number of people can do and I'm proud to be part of that special family. I know that a challenge is what drives me and that I want more. I know that this has been a great ride, but there are many great moments ahead of me – and I'll be up to them.

My hope is that you will take that same challenge. Your experiences may be somewhat different from mine, but the net effect will be much the same. It is an experience unique to you, but, as it does to all of us in "the family," it will make you a different person, in a very positive way. I guarantee it.

Photo: Lee Gruenfeld

Mike Reilly, the "Voice of Ironman"

In the Arena

It is not the critic who counts: not the man who points out how the strong man stumbles, or where the doer of deeds could have done them better. The credit belongs to the man who is actually in the arena, whose face is marred by dust and sweat and blood; who strives valiantly; who errs, who comes up short again and again, because there is no effort without error and shortcoming; but who does actually strive to do the deeds; who knows great enthusiasms, the great devotions; who spends himself in a worthy cause; who at the best knows in the end the triumph of high achievement, and who at the worst, if he fails, at least fails while daring

*greatly, so that his place shall never be with those cold and timid souls
who neither know victory nor defeat.*

Theodore Roosevelt

*For of all sad words of tongue or pen,
The saddest are these: "It might have been."*

John Greenleaf Whittier

I've spent the last 15 years involved in the sport of triathlon, as a racer, a coach and as an observer of the sport. During that time I've experienced thrills and disappointments. I've been strong and have watched from the sidelines with an injury. I've seen people exceed their goals and seen them fall short. I've noticed fear etched on faces pre-race and seen pure exhilaration and relief at the finish line. It seems I've seen it all.

But the one thing I've never experienced is a triathlete, regardless of his or her personal situation, saying "I wish I hadn't done it."

Triathlon, especially the long-distance variety, is a risky venture. We crash our bikes, we get dehydrated, we overtrain and get sick and we spend our share of time with a physical therapist or an orthopedist.
But the most significant risk is not that we might perform poorly or get hurt. It's that we fail to try, that we spend our lives saying "I think I could have" or "I wish I had."

Some risks are worth taking. Others are foolish or ego-driven. I'm here to tell you that trying to become an Ironman is one of the most worthwhile and potentially rewarding endeavors you're likely to take in your lifetime. Once you've done it, once you're "in the arena," you'll never look back and wish you hadn't tried.

So let's go. As Sherlock Holmes used to put it: "The game is afoot!"

It is never too late to be what you might have been.
George Eliot

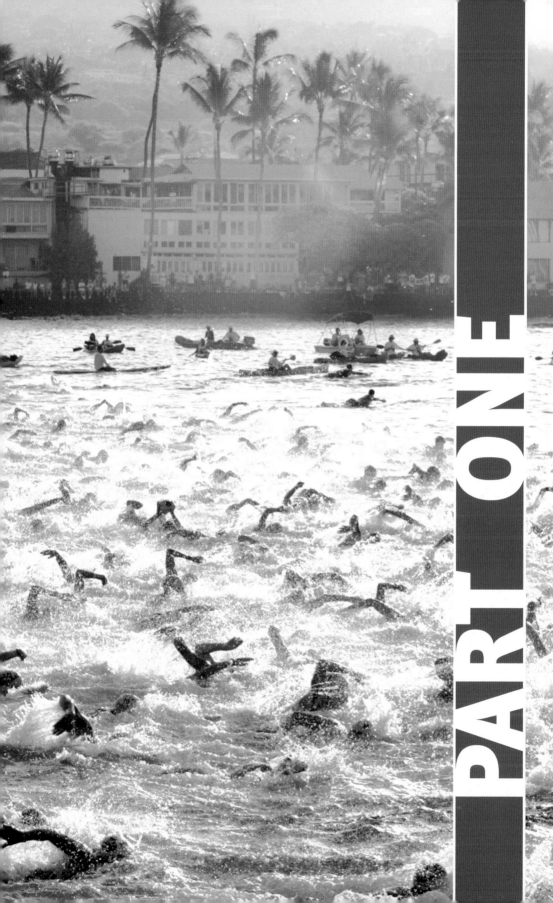

PART I — FIRST THINGS FIRST

First you jump off the cliff and you build wings on the way down.
Ray Bradbury

1 Getting Started

If you want to get ahead...
get started.
Anonymous

At one time, each of us was sitting on the sidelines watching. And for each of us, something or somebody inspired us to stand up and declare, "I want to be one of those people." And when we made that decision and set the goal, we stepped into new territory, believing that the reward of great achievement was worth the risks, which were largely unknown.

The commitment to this big a goal can be a life-altering experience. From this moment on, when someone asks you how you spend your off-hours, you won't say "I do triathlons." Rather your answer will be: "I am a triathlete."

To be successful in this world takes some special characteristics:

- You need to focus on the goal with single-mindedness while keeping your life in balance – a very tricky feat in the best of circumstances.

- You must be willing to accept and learn from failure because we don't always get it right.

- You need to have support from your loved ones. Your sacrifices will become theirs and they need to feel some reward from this venture as well.

- You must be able to face fear. Activities such as swimming in rough water or biking on slick streets can be very scary, but shouldn't be an excuse for not trying.

You'll walk around with chlorine bleached hair, saddle sores and ugly toes. Your medical bills may increase to the point that your insurance company starts asking questions while your bank account shows some decreases. And you'll develop an unusually close bond with your UPS/FedEx delivery guy and local bike shop mechanic.

But none of this matters nor is even remembered when you cross the finish line, having done what you set out to do, knowing that you've achieved something rare and wonderful:

You are an Ironman!

2 Do I Need a Coach?

On the surface, the benefit of using a coach seems fairly obvious: if you are serious about competing, then having someone with a lot of experience help you achieve your race goals is a no-brainer, assuming you can afford it.

But there are other, less obvious reasons to seek professional guidance.

• Let's say you've raced successfully for years. You probably think you've got a working formula, and why mess with success? However, as we age and the body racks up more wear and tear, the workouts that served us so well in the past may need some modification in order to keep us in the game and performing well. Whereas you might be loath to change that intense Wednesday brick that has been a standard for years, a savvy coach might be able to make subtle changes that will get you just as fast and strong, but with somewhat less damage than the old "tried and true."

Hard to believe from this picture, but Roch Frey and Paul Huddle are two of the best coaches in the business

- Another reason is to help you come back from an injury, which can be a risky and unfamiliar journey. Putting yourself in the hands of a coach who is knowledgeable in this area relieves you of trying to figure out: "Am I doing enough? Am I doing too much? Will I be ready for the big race?" Using a coach you trust and following his advice in your comeback will let you focus all your energy on the workouts he gives you rather than on second guessing yourself.

- Your personal style is a consideration as well, especially if you're driven toward a competitive goal but are a bit of a follower. By "follower" I mean that you tend to fall into other people's workouts, maybe doing a hard 80-mile ride with the group when what you really needed was a 40-mile recovery ride. If this is you, a coach can help you resist outside influence and stick to a plan that you know is the right one to follow. (It can be a graceful way out, too: "Would love to, but my coach says...")

- Another good reason to use a coach is if you find you're getting stale. You know the workouts you need, you know how to "plan the work and work the plan," but it's become routine, and you're having trouble getting inspired enough to have a breakthrough race. Get a coach, let him shake up the routine a bit and present you with some new training challenges, and watch your performances improve.

On the other hand, is there a time when coaching is not necessarily the right option for you? Probably.

Some athletes like to do well at races but, if they're honest with themselves, realize that they are more interested in having a good time during training than in getting serious about a personal record performance. After all, the 80-mile group ride is probably going to be more fun than a recovery ride. There's nothing wrong with this attitude, but paying a coach for a workout schedule that you find burdensome and won't follow is a waste of money (and will not foster an enjoyable relationship with the coach).

Another reason for passing on a coach might be that you have a personal situation or particular type of injury that will keep your schedule erratic for a while. When you don't have the ability to set reasonable, achievable training goals, investing in coaching doesn't make much sense.

If you do decide to get some professional assistance, keep in mind that there are a couple of options in coaching available. Personalized coaching will get you your own coach, who will work with you face-to-face on your specific goals and design a program tailored to your individual needs. Online coaching programs are another option that is becoming increasingly popular. These are less expensive than a personal coach, and are especially well-suited to preparation for a specific race or type of race (e.g., an Ironman or Half Ironman/70.3).

If you decide to use a coach, be sure to select one who will:

- Ensure that your goals are reasonable and tailored to your specific skills and capabilities

- Create a structured program that you can easily work into your life

- Carefully monitor your progress and recommend adjustments

PART TWO

PART II — THE ROAD MAP

Three veterans who know their way to the finish line: Jim Adamson, Bill Riley & Bruce Buchanan

Photo: Tim Carlson

It's a line you have to cross to understand.
(Unknown Ironman athlete)

3 Analyzing Last Season to Have a Better Next Season

When you find the holidays fast approaching, that can only mean one thing: Last season is "in the books" and next season is about to take over your life. Because of the popularity of our sport, you've probably already had to commit to your big races next year, so you know the task ahead of you. While you're enjoying your down-time (and please remember to take some down-time), spend a little of it reviewing your last season, taking from it what you can to make the next one even better.

(If you're a newbie and don't yet *have* a last season, save this chapter for next year!)

In analyzing your past performances, approach it from a positive perspective. You may have had a Dream Season or you may have fallen a little short of a few goals. In the former case, you'll want to continue what made you successful and make changes or additions to your training while not tampering with the proven success factors. In the latter case, don't spend precious time beating yourself up. Some things that happen on the race course can be explained and some simply cannot. Focus on those you understand and let the others go.
Whether you're analyzing a great season and working to improve from there (after all, the competitors you whomped all season don't want to let that happen again) or you're needing to make some changes that will improve your chances of accomplishing next season's goals, here are some things to think about:

1) **If you use the same recipe, you get the same bread.**
   Make some changes to your training and evaluate the results. This may take some experimenting, but you've got the time if you're planning now.
   For example, if you haven't been including drills in each of your swim sessions, you might want to start. You'll also get great benefit from replacing one of your run days with a drill session, where you train your body with better running technique.

2) If what you're doing isn't working, do something else.

If you got sick during your Ironman race, start experimenting with your nutrition. If you ran out of steam at Mile 18 of the run, include more focused long run training including a couple of longer transition runs (bricks). If you were so nervous on race morning that you threw up before you got to the start line, race more. If you got to the start line beat-up and burned-out, race less. If you found that you did the training all season but it was not really focused or enjoyable, look at your priorities. Maybe this isn't the right time in your life for such goals.

Photo: John Segesta

3) "More" is not the same as "better."

Coming off a season where you missed a target, the temptation is to punish yourself by piling on the miles, which quickly become nothing but junk miles. It's like a golfer on the driving range hitting hundreds of balls without practicing anything specific, and therefore missing a good deal of the benefit of all that work. Quality over quantity is a proven success factor in our business. Make sure every workout has a purpose and be committed to that before you step out the door to start the session. If you're not working on something, you're just working.

4) Be honest with yourself about your goals.

Did you win all your races, but never leave your local area and play with the "big boys?" It's great fun being the big fish in a little pond and if your goal is to be the local hero, then by all means go for it. But if your goals are on a larger scale, you need to get out and test yourself. Don't be intimidated. Enter some big races and see what happens. On the other hand, if you find you're exclusively racing big, high-profile races, take the pressure off once in awhile and race locally. You'll probably go home with hardware and have fun with the hometown crowd.

5) Be realistic, too.

I had a new client once who told me he planned on doing his Ironman in 10:30. When I asked him about his plan to accomplish that, he hadn't really given it a lot of thought. So I took him through the goal setting process: "How fast do you think you can do the swim?" To which he replied, "1:20." For the bike, he figured 6:00 and for the run, 4:15. Without transitions, he was already at 11:35.

This little exercise quickly brought him back to earth and we proceeded with a more achievable goal.

When setting your time goal, make sure you've thought it through!

Whatever last season was for you, use it to your advantage this season.

4 Setting the Race Calendar

Since you've now completed the task of analyzing your last season in anticipation of having a better next season, it's time to start thinking about specific races of interest. With big races filling so quickly, you've probably already registered for your key race(s) and are starting to think through an appropriate training schedule and supporting race schedule that will work for you.

You may have heard the terms A, B and C races:

> **A:** top priority (goal race)
> **B:** key to preparation for race A
> **C:** training

If you're a candidate for Kona, the Ironman World Championships, you can read the above as:

> **A:** Kona
> **B:** qualifying race
> **C:** all other races

Prioritizing your schedule into A, B and C races is not a new concept and is easy to do. But I'd like to present a few ideas that I hope will provoke some additional thought about your C races.

1. We triathletes seem to have an obsession about comparing our performances from year to year. There are some pros and cons to that. When we perform better, we think we're pretty hot stuff and it's a big confidence booster. If it goes the other way, for whatever reason, we can be very hard on ourselves, wasting a lot of time and energy on "Why?"

   That problem can be solved by entering some new events for your C races. Go race some fresh venues where you have no past results for comparison. These are training races and your goals can be accomplished on any course. Go have some new adventures instead of the same old tests.

2. Your C races are training days, which implies that you will be training right through them with no rest and taper. Your legs will be tired and your focus may be elsewhere. This is the time to "park your ego" because you're likely going to get beaten, perhaps by competitors whom you have beaten in the past. For a C race, the mark of success should not be winning or besting an old rival, but rather accomplishing the specific goal you set for that day (e.g., running strong off the bike). The key to a productive C race is to keep in mind the overall strategy for the season – preparing for a great A race, not winning the C race. And because you're training through it, you want to get right back to training afterwards, so trashing yourself on tired legs with an all-out effort to win will probably leave you needing some additional recovery time...which defeats the whole purpose!

3. The timing of a C race in relation to your A race can be critical. I'll preface this by reminding you that what works for one athlete will not work for all athletes. So the following are simply considerations:

   - Many times there is a good race three or four weeks out which looks perfect as a final test of your Build/Peak Phase* before you head into your taper. Putting the "cap" on your training with this sort of race works beautifully for many athletes. But there is a huge mental component to keep in mind as well: If for some reason the race doesn't go as well as you expected, it's possible to lose the confidence you were so carefully building. At this point in the schedule, there's no time to regroup and regain that confidence. This race, unlike other C races, is not a learning race. It's a confidence booster, giving you the mental edge you'll need for your upcoming A race. So think it through before you sign up.

   - If the race that looks so perfect is 4-6 weeks before your A race, this presents another consideration. Again, this may work perfectly for some athletes. For others, recovery may be an issue

---

* In case you're not familiar with this term, check out the definition in Chapter 7. Briefly, it's the "big work" phase of the training leading up to a specific race.

to think about. If the race is a Half Ironman/70.3 and you're using it as an intense training day, your body is going to be stressed and will need a good recovery. What is problematic about this is that the recovery time will come during the key Build/Peak Phase of your Ironman training for the upcoming A race. So you need to consider the trade-offs – a good race-intensity workout versus time out of the training schedule for recovery. Your call. Only you will know what works for you.

One final thought: if last season wasn't one you're still talking about, mix it up next year. Try some new races and some new strategies and let your A race next year be one you'll be bragging about long into the future.

5   The Course

You've signed up and paid your entry fees. Your training plan is in place and you're "good to go" with your Ironman training. But not all Ironman races are created equal. It all depends on The Course: *where* it is and *what* it is.

For example, Kona is on the tropical island of Hawaii, which means that weather conditions will be a major factor. Lake Placid, home of the 1980 Winter Olympic Games, is in the Adirondack Mountains, so you're going to be facing hilly terrain. Your carefully planned program for Ironman training should take into consideration the particular course challenges you'll be faced with on race day.

Step number one is to go to the race website and study the course. Most websites now provide bike and run course profile maps. Study those carefully to get an understanding of elevation changes. In many cases you can get information about likely weather conditions, including race day weather in past years.

Step number two is to use that information to build a training program specific to that Ironman course.

Terrain

If you'll be racing a flat course such as Ironman Florida, you'll want to spend plenty of riding time on the flats, down on your aerobars. Flat courses can be very hard on your body because you aren't forced to change positions as you are on a hilly or technical course. During training, teach yourself to get out of the aerobars and to stand and pedal a few strokes on a regular basis. This will let you use other muscles and relieve the ones that are being overtaxed from many hours in one position.

If you're heading for a hilly course such as Ironman Canada, it goes without saying that you should head for the hills in training. Learn to

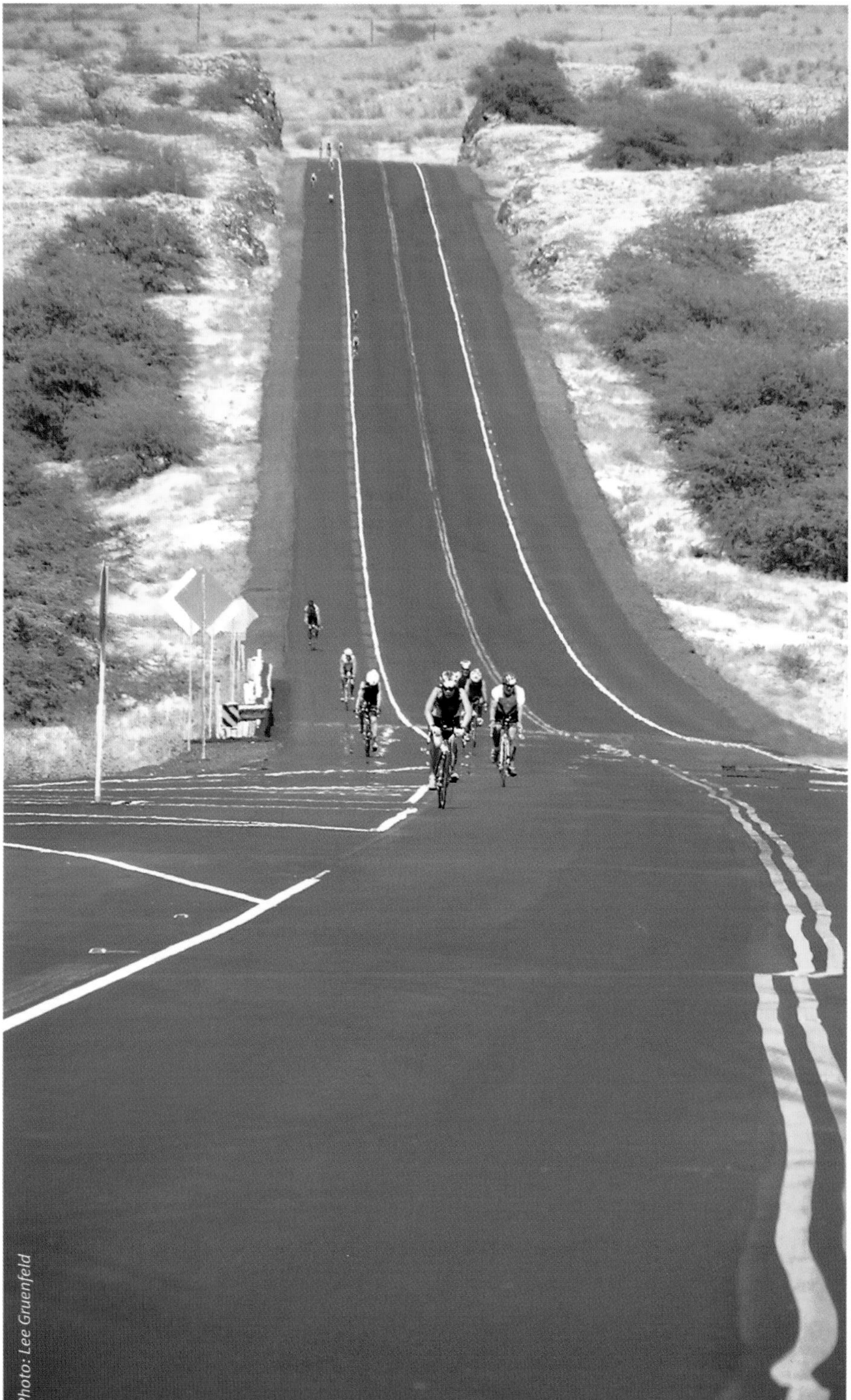

Photo: Lee Gruenfeld

be efficient spinning up the hills so that you have something left in your legs at the top and can put it in a harder gear and get going rather than have to spend time recovering.

Some Ironman courses are more technical than others, having lots of turns and requiring more bike handling skills. This is especially true of some of the European races. If this is what you're going to be tackling, riding with a group is a good way to develop bike handling skills. But word of caution: Stay out of your aerobars when riding in a pack. The aerobar position is not a safe place to be when riding in a crowd, because you're less able to react quickly should a fellow rider make it necessary.

Weather Conditions

This challenge is a little trickier because, except for Kona where it's always hot, always humid and usually windy, it's a bit difficult to predict what you'll face on race day. Go prepared for anything, which means taking cold and wet weather clothes so they're available if needed. Also prepare mentally for the possibility of miserable conditions so that it doesn't become a major negative for you if it should happen. The folks who accepted the freezing and wet conditions in Ironman Wisconsin in 2006 were the ones who had a good day. Those under-dressed and angry about their bad luck were the ones who had a really tough go. Same was true in Wisconsin the prior year, except that it was one of the hottest IMs ever instead of one of the coldest.

At any Ironman it can get hot, especially by run time, and that's something you can train for. During the hot weather wherever you're training, don't go out for an early morning run hoping to avoid the heat. Wait for midday or late afternoon when it's at the peak of misery.

Wind can also be a factor at any Ironman. During training, you often have the option of sailing with a tail wind or turning into a fierce head wind. Which do you think will prepare you better for your upcoming race?

Other thoughts on how to prepare specifically for your chosen Ironman course:

- If at all possible, make a trip to the course 6-8 weeks before the race when you're in your peak training time. Make it a weekend training camp, riding the course on Saturday and running part of it on Sunday. The objective is not to hammer and see how fast you can go but rather to study the course, to learn how you'll ride and run it smartly and efficiently on race day.

- If you have a CompuTrainer, it's very likely that your particular Ironman bike course is available for downloading. If so, take advantage of that and train on it.

- Once you've studied the course (in person or on the website), break both the bike and run course into small, manageable pieces. On race day, never think about 112 biking miles or 26.2 running miles. Rather focus only on the next section in your plan.

Any Ironman is a challenge. But knowing The Course can give you an edge.

6 Allocating Your Workout Time for a Great Season

Ever find yourself fretting about how to fit your workouts into your busy life?

A triathlete needs to swim, bike and run. We can also all use some time in the weight room and stretching, and don't forget the need to rest in order for your body to fully benefit from all the work. These are time-demanding activities, and trying to balance them with such "non-negotiables" as work, family obligations, pool availability and daylight hours is enough to stress even the non-Type A's among us (if there is such a thing).

So let's look at those areas where we do have some control and talk about a few ways to best allocate time.

Swim-Bike-Run

Most of us are guilty of emphasizing our strongest discipline. After all, it's much more fun to be the lead swimmer in the fast lane at the Masters workout than to fight getting dropped in the group bike ride. However, come race day, getting out of the water first gives only momentary pleasure which quickly fades as all those fast bikers go zooming by. This makes the case for planning your schedule with an emphasis on your weaker discipline(s). When doing your weekly schedule, plan the workouts in your weaker disciplines first, giving them your prime time (when you'll have a group to push you; when you'll have the most energy; when there's the least chance of it being canceled). Then follow up with plans in your stronger disciplines.

Another consideration in allocating time for your swim-bike-run workouts is the old truism: Ironman is all about the run. Believe it now or learn it later: it's not over until the run and the fastest runner will nearly always win the day. (There are a few examples where that's not the case, but Normann Stadler and Natascha Badmann are the exceptions, not the rule.) So, whether we like running or not, run training should be key in the workout plan.

The long run will obviously be the most time-consuming of your run workouts. Planning this on Sunday, following the long ride Saturday, fits well into the working person's schedule and is a very good training tool: back-to-back long bike/run.

Also plan to do a very short run each time you finish a bike ride. This is great race training and takes very little time.

Because distance is your thing, long bike rides are going to take a large chunk of time and it's usually not possible to do them on a work day. As mentioned above, Saturday is a very good day for this, and if you're not up for a solo workout, you'll find lots of company if you live in or visit an area where there are other triathletes or cyclists.

In trying to find an effective allocation of workout time, some triathletes have found success with the following strategy:

As you get closer to your big race, plan some "discipline weeks." For example, one week you will focus on running, with very minimal bike and swim sessions. Follow this by a big swim week, running and biking very, very lightly. Finish with a focused bike week, where running and swimming take low priority.

If you choose to do this, be sure to take into account your personal vulnerability to injury. This is especially applicable during the run week if you have a history of problems following extended run training.

Weight Work and Stretching

Although these aren't among the "big three," they are very important to your overall performance and general good health.

Stretching can be a daily activity done at home at any hour. To avoid boredom it can be done in front of the television or stereo, or while talking with your family. Get into a routine so that it becomes an integral part of the day and not just something else you have to struggle to fit in.

Weight work should be planned according to the time of the year. During the race season, you need very little time in the gym and it can even be another at-home activity, if you have the equipment and the discipline. Two to three sessions per week of less than an hour will give you what you need. In the off-season you can increase your weight workouts as a nice change of pace from extended swimming, biking and running.

Rest

Triathletes are often reluctant to take a full day of rest or a recovery week, although both are critical to a successful season. Growth in strength and endurance doesn't occur when you train; it occurs afterward, when you rest. As the very first step in building your weekly schedule, plan your rest and recovery. Then build your workouts around that, planning your weaker discipline workouts first. For (a lot) more on this critical topic, see Chapter 17.

7 Periodization — Make It Work for You

The training we do creates stress on the body. When given the appropriate rest following the stress, the body adapts, becoming stronger and fitter. If we don't vary the exercise level — if every workout is a hammer fest all year round — adaptation could "plateau," overall fitness can even decrease, and the likelihood of injury increases. Mental staleness can result as well, leading to burn-out and a great deal of frustration.

Periodization is a fancy name for a concept that has been a staple of athletes in many sports for years. Let's take a look at an example of how a triathlete, looking ahead to a new season, might apply the principles of training in phases — "periodization" — in the quest to become an Ironman. The following time frames assume you're aiming for an early-season Ironman, but you can easily adapt them for whatever your goal Ironman is.

Base Phase (November – December)

The objective of base training is to build the foundation for more intensive training to come. It allows the musculoskeletal system time to build a tolerance for hard work, and it teaches the muscles to burn fat as their primary fuel. Skipping this phase is akin to building a house without the foundation.

The core workout policy of this phase is low intensity exercise with increasing volume to build endurance. All work should be done in the aerobic zone: long sustained effort with a low heart rate. No speed work, no intervals and no hill repeats.

Build Phase (January – February)

Once the foundation is built, your body should be able to take advantage of some increased intensity without risking injury. The emphasis on endurance should be decreased while you build in some anaerobic work and test yourself with speed work, intervals and hill repeats.

Peak/Taper/Race Phase (March – April)

This is where you put it all together, culminating with your goal race. In training for an Ironman, you'll need to add some endurance back in while keeping the intensity. This is a very stressful period and should not be maintained for more than 3-4 weeks before you start your taper three weeks before race day.

Following a recovery period after your race, you can then return to the Build Phase and start working towards the next goal race.

The above is one example which fits well with an early season race. If your schedule calls for your first race coming later in the year, you can make adjustments. There are a few principles, however, that should guide any scenario:

- The less training/racing experience you have, the longer your Base Phase should be. Also, if you're coming off the previous season with an injury or chronic pain, lengthening this phase will give your body more time to rebuild.
- None of this will pay off as you intend if you don't allow for recovery time for your body to adapt and grow stronger. In your weekly schedule, be sure to be fully rested before doing a hard workout. In your monthly schedule, three hard training weeks followed by an easier "recovery" week is a good guide.
- Very easy workouts frequently work better for recovery than total rest. But this is a fine line and going over it with further stress will be totally counterproductive.

Many athletes enjoy racing during the off-season, which can easily work into a periodization plan. The Base Phase is a good time to do a winter marathon if you can commit to it being a training race and not a personal record. Save that personal record marathon for the Peak/Race Phase.

Running races of 5K/10K/Half Marathons fit well into the Build Phase where you can test yourself with a challenging goal. Sprint triathlons can be fun anytime as long as you adjust your race plan from "going for a personal record" to "racing with the kids," depending on what time of year it is.

PART THREE

Photo: WTC/Ironman

Diana Hassel
finishing strong

PART III — TRAINING THE BODY

I sweat blood in training so I don't have to in the race.
Steve Prefontaine

Photo: John Segesta

8 Faster Is Better: Swimming

We triathletes are always looking to better our overall race times, but we often fall into the trap of "wishing it so." To improve in any of the three disciplines you have to set a goal, follow a plan and continually test yourself against the goal. It's hard work, but the end result can be very rewarding.

Has this ever happened to you? Having spent your life keeping fit, your ripped body looks very cool in your skimpy swimsuit. Then you find yourself in a swim lane next to a fellow whose beer gut practically covers his Speedo, but he's out-swimming you. What's up with that?

The swim is far more about technique than pure fitness and brute force. It doesn't hurt to be fit and strong, but you'll never swim fast without proper technique. So swim training to get faster will necessarily have to include drills along with interval work. Drills can easily be included in the warm-up. Don't try to do them on a pre-set interval or you'll get sloppy as you try to make the interval. Take plenty of time and get the full benefit.

The first step in this improvement plan is to find a starting point. This can be done with a time-trial workout, such as the following:

1 1000 warm-up swim/kick/pull/drill
2 10x50 drill/swim
3 Time trials
   (Take plenty of rest after each effort – Get your heart rate down)
   1000 time trial
   200 time trial
   100 time trial
   200 cool down

The results of your three time trials become your starting point. The next step is to set a realistic goal: how much do you want to take off these times in your next time trial in four weeks and what pace must you swim to make those times? This becomes your goal. Now you need a plan that includes swimming 3 days a week with the following types of workouts:

1) Technique/Endurance

Workout:	Sets of 300/400/500/600/800/1000
Focus:	Distance per stroke
Sample Main Set:	4x500 Keep a steady stroke count
	Last 25 of each 100, 1 stroke less
Key to Successful Workout:	Continually check your form

2) Short Interval Work

Workout:	Sets of 50/75/100
Focus:	All-out intensity with lots of rest
Sample Main Set:	20x50 5 sec. faster than 1000 goal pace. Take enough rest to get your heart rate down before starting the next interval
Key to Successful Workout:	Stress your body. Get comfortable with discomfort

3) Long Interval Work

Workout:	Sets of 200/300/400/500
Focus:	Controlled speed with short rest periods

Sample Main Set:	5x200 descending each 200 or 3x400 descending through each 400
Key to Successful Workout:	Don't let your form fall apart as you increase speed (use stroke count as your guide) and build strength by keeping the rest breaks short

Chasing a goal like this can be stressful, so try to have a little fun with it. Each week throw in some stroke work, do a little racing against a lane mate, dolphin on your back for some ab work, play some GOLF (add up your time and strokes and shoot for a low score) or try the "wet version" of fartleks: During a long set, speed up for a few strokes every once in awhile. Once a week, do a workout that includes 10x100, with 15-20 seconds rest, at your 1000 goal pace. This will help get you used to the pace you'll need to keep during your next time trial.

In four weeks, duplicate the Time Trial workout, using all you've learned during the month's training. As I said earlier, it's hard work, but on race day you'll find it was a price worth paying.

God gives talent. Work transforms talent into genius.
Anna Pavlova

Rich Clark on his way to yet
another of many course records

9 Faster Is Better: Biking

We've been talking about the ongoing quest to post faster race results and the necessity of setting goals and working a plan in order to accomplish this. We focused on improving the swim over a 4-week period. Now let's talk about what happens after we get out of the water.

The first thing to keep in mind is that we're not training for the Tour de France. We're training for an event where the fastest bike split of the day is *not* the goal. Have you ever heard a triathlete bragging after a race about his fast bike split, only to discover his run time was nearly the same as his bike time? This is not podium material. The bike goal for a triathlete involves efficiency as much as speed. It's counterproductive to hammer the bike for every ounce of speed if it leaves you unable to put together a quality run. Therefore, a plan to post a faster bike time must take into account the run and will involve the following:

1	Technique
2	Endurance
3	Strength and Power
4	Focus
5	Buying Speed

Technique

Although we're not training for the Tour, we should learn from Lance that spinning with a high cadence is an excellent strategy in an endurance event. Not only does spinning cause less fatigue, but it fairly closely simulates your leg turnover in the run. Both of these will pay off big time after T2.

- On a trainer: After a warm-up, start increasing your cadence to 110-120 rpm or until you're no longer able to either hold your upper body still or keep your butt in the saddle. When you reach that high cadence where you're able to keep your form, applying steady power through the entire 360° of each pedal stroke, continue for one minute, then spin easy at lower rpm for 2 minutes and repeat.
- On the road: Use a medium gear and get your cadence up to around 100 keeping your form. Maintain for 30 minutes and then spin easy for another 30 and repeat.

Endurance

It's important to keep your form through the end of the race. Including these workouts in your long rides will force you to work on form when you're not fresh.
- During the middle of a 2-3 hour ride, include a steady interval, riding at about your Olympic distance race pace. Start with 10 minutes and work up to 30.
- When your rides get really long (4-7 hours), do the work at your Half Ironman pace. Start with 20 minutes and work up to 40.

Strength and Power

The off-season is the perfect time to become a gym rat, using weight work to build your body into a stronger biking machine. As your first race gets closer, you'll want to move into more cycling-specific workouts, such as the following:

- One of the riding styles that will help increase speed is "staying aero" — remaining down on your aerobars to reduce wind resistance — so train yourself to be able to do this even when you encounter rolling hills or are hit by big winds. Find an area that is slighty uphill, get into a fairly large gear, stay aero and — smoothly and forcefully, with a strong pedal stroke down and a good upward pull — ride that way for 20-30 seconds. Take a 3-minute recovery and do it again.

- If you've done a good job of base-building, try this one: On a moderate hill, stay seated pushing a large gear at 50-60 rpm. Continue for 5-10 minutes. Do only a couple of these and get plenty of rest in between.

Focus

This component of a fast bike time is perhaps the most important but least appreciated piece of the equation. If two racers are equal in all the above-mentioned areas, the more focused of the two will be the winner every time. Staying focused for long periods of time when you're in pain is very difficult and needs to be learned. Time trials are a good training tool for this, as well as a good measuring stick of your progress.

Find a 20-40 minute route with very little traffic and no stop lights (or use a trainer) and hold as hard an effort as you can maintain through to the end. Keep your head in the game, concentrating on technique from start to finish, and you've just gone a long way towards developing the ability to focus. (More about this in Part IV.)

Buying Speed

Thankfully, there are some areas where you can get "free" speed, which can be bought with no additional training time or physical effort on race day. Anything that makes you more aero will result in less wind resistance and, therefore, more speed, or less expenditure of effort for the same speed. As well, proper fit on the bike will allow you to get the most out of each pedal stroke and will pay big dividends in power and speed, not to mention comfort. Even if you can't afford to ride a top-of-the-line bike, you can make sure that you're getting the most from what you've got by being properly fitted by someone with expertise in this area.

Becoming a faster, more efficient biker is an ongoing project for everyone. There are no magic bullets that will do the trick overnight. However, if you build a training program that combines the proper distances with intervals and recovery and focuses on technique, the result will not only be a better bike time but a better quality run. And that will make you podium worthy.

Photo: John Segesta

Teresa Rider, 2006 45-49
Ironman World Champion

10 Faster Is Better: Running

A successful Ironman Triathlon is all about the run.

Sounds like a fairly suspect statement considering you have to get through a 2.4 mile swim and 112 miles on the bike before you even put on your running shoes.

If you look at the results of any Ironman race, any age group, either gender, you will find an instructive pattern. The top three finishers in the age group might have had the fastest bike splits, but often they didn't. They will for certain have had the three fastest run splits. And if you search further down the age group, you'll nearly always find a few racers posting blazingly fast bike times followed by painfully slow run times.

An Ironman race is all about the run.

Yes, in 2004 we saw Normann Stadler win Ironman with an astonishing breakaway on the bike, but Kona historians are quick to remind us of John Howard's 1981 win. The year before, he had shattered the bike record only to fade to 3rd on the run. To get the win in 1981, he backed off 35 minutes on the bike and, with that more conservative pace, improved his run by fifty minutes over 1980 and took top honors. Winning Ironman on the bike has been done, but not often enough for we mere mortals to plan our race strategy on it. Therefore, Ironman training is all about conditioning your body to run well off the bike.

So let's proceed with our discussion of that all-important last discipline. Although your Ironman run time will be affected both by the conditions and how well you manage the bike leg, there are some general training guidelines that can vastly improve your odds of having a faster run regardless.

Use Your Head

Of the three disciplines, running is perhaps the one with the most striking mind-body connection. How many times have you seen an athlete cross the finish line strong only to fall into the arms of a volunteer and be carried off to the medical tent, literally unable to take even one more step? That's a perfect example of mind over body. Your mind is a powerful weapon that can work for or against you. Training it to work in your favor is the first step toward a good Ironman run.

- Put yourself in tough training conditions. Every time you complete a session where you feel you've earned bragging rights, you're stronger mentally and it will build on itself. The next time out, you'll remember that workout and know you can handle something just a little tougher. By race day, you'll have an entire library of tough experiences that have your confidence at an all-time high.
- Take your body where your mind wants to go. Your mind has you running like a gazelle; however, sometimes your body is not so willing and you slip into a slow shuffle. I'll share my secret here for

helping my mind take over when my weary body refuses to cooperate: I mentally flash back to a movie called "Endurance," the story of Ethiopian runner Haile Gebrselassie. Parts of this movie show him running through the African countryside with an effortless stride and feeling nothing but pure joy. For me, this is the picture in my mind's eye that focuses and re-energizes me. Find your own inspiration or go to your local video store and rent mine.

- Follow all your long rides with a short (20-30 min.) run. On the bike, concentrate on good technique and your nutrition, both of which will pay off on the run. This transition run needn't be fast, just strong, getting your legs working and establishing your running rhythm as quickly as possible.

- As the three Ironman distances are too long to do consecutively during training and would require too much recovery time, you can simulate it instead by doing back-to-back workouts. For example: On Saturday, do a long ride, following by a short transition run. On Sunday, do a long swim, followed by a long run.

- You want to train to run the distance, but running long distances can be very tough on your body, especially if you have a vulnerability that tends to act up with long distance training. So try splitting your long run into two runs. For example: run for 2 hours in the morning and another 45 minutes in the afternoon. You'll still get the training benefit, but you'll be protecting your body.

The Need for Speed

It's natural for someone training for an Ironman to feel that longer is better. Although the long run is a necessary workout, it's not enough when you're looking to improve your time. If you train your body with plenty of long slow runs, on race day you'll do a long, slow run. You need to get your body used to the stress of some intensity over the long haul.

- Enter **shorter races**. Doing sprint or Olympic triathlons will force you to push at your top end in all three disciplines. If you haven't been doing them, you'll be amazed at how tough it is, so you'll be building mental strength at the same time.

- **Hill repeats** — working hard on the way up and recovering on the way down — are speed work in disguise. You can do these on trails or the road, short bursts or longer pulls. Have some fun while still getting in a good, hard workout that will improve your overall speed.

- **Mile repeats** — a strong mile followed by recovery — force you to run at your maximum sustainable pace. Strive to maintain an even pace throughout and do each mile at the same pace (about your 10K pace) with a rest interval of half the work time. Do 3-5 of these per session.
- During your run, include some **accelerations** where you build up from your regular pace to top speed and maintain it for 20-30 seconds. This will train your legs for flats and downhills as well as for quickening your pace to reel in your competitors one by one on race day.
- **Tempo runs** provide both a mental and a physical workout because you're training your body to operate at intensity for a long period of time. Aim for about 15 seconds per mile slower than your 10K pace and hold that for 20-40 minutes. In the beginning, if you need to break it up, do 5 minute tempo sessions with no more than 1 minute of active rest (easy jogging).

Patience Is a Virtue

Of the three disciplines, running can be the one that most often hurts you, especially hard, fast running. It's unrealistic and potentially harmful to expect to see a quick, dramatic improvement in your run times. But if you put in the work, you will eventually reap the rewards. Don't be afraid to push hard, but pay close attention to your body and what it's telling you during and after the workouts.

A Race Day Commitment to a Strong Run

Perhaps the biggest contributor to an Ironman athlete having a fast run on race day is the commitment to it, which can easily fade in the late hours of the race. It's very easy to fall into some "good enough" thinking: *All I have to do is make it to the finish line. It's good enough.* While there's truth to that, giving up on your running strategy and just getting to the end will probably leave you with a gnawing in your gut that you could have done better. There are no guarantees in an Ironman race, but believing that *It's all about the run,* training with that belief in mind and holding onto it for dear life when it gets really tough on race day, will tremendously increase your odds of a satisfying race, one you'll be very proud of because you know you gave it your very best.

11 The Brick/Transition Run

If it was easy, it would be easy.
(Unknown)

When an athlete decides to expand from a single discipline into three and become a triathlete, he or she will very shortly learn of "The Brick" and probably wonder where the term originated. The most common first guess is the most obvious – your legs feel like bricks when you get off the bike and try to take your first running steps. Or maybe it's because you're laying one workout on the other (the run on top of the bike) as you would with bricks. One rumor has it that it was created by duathlete Matt Brick. Regardless of its origin, the brick has become a standard in the triathlon world.

Some triathletes train for the run the way they might for a pure marathon. But the unique thing about the Ironman marathon run is that it follows the swim and the bike, so by the time you get to the run portion of your race, you're working on very tired legs. Therefore, doesn't it make sense to do much of your run training on tired legs? Hence, the brick, or "transition run," another training method where you run following a bike ride.

The objective of this type of double workout is twofold:
- To train your mind and your legs to get into a running rhythm as quickly as possible (Transition Run)
- To train your tired body to keep good form as you get more and more fatigued (Brick)

Here are a few workout ideas that will accomplish these goals while adding some variety to your training schedule:
- Each time you complete a long ride, put on your running shoes and go for a short run (15-30 minutes), focusing on getting into the rhythm quickly.
- When you're looking for a short workout, do a quick bike/run workout at race pace.

- A mid-distance workout (bike 3 hours/ run 1 hour) will work on both getting your rhythm quickly and keeping your form as you tire.
- A longer workout can be split, giving you the same benefits without the risk inherent in a long run (bike an hour/ run an hour/ bike an hour/ run an hour)
- A modified form of a long brick is a two-day workout, doing a long ride on Saturday followed by a long run on Sunday. (This is one case where a long transition is acceptable!) You're getting the benefit of a long run on tired legs with far less risk of injury and it doesn't require the same level of recovery as a long traditional brick workout.

When doing a double workout, you needn't push through the transition from bike to run at race pace. Taking a few minutes to safely stow your bike or grab a banana is fine. If you're out on the run in 5-10 minutes, you're getting the benefit. It's also worth reminding the Type A's among us that it's not necessary to do these sessions all year 'round. Take the off-season to enjoy and improve the three disciplines and save the bricks for the in-season, race-specific training.

Have fun and get your run stronger with these workouts but keep in mind that a long brick workout puts additional stress on your body and will require additional recovery time. Plan your schedule to allow for the recovery and you'll see the benefits out on the race course.

12 Final Tune-up for Ironman

You're very close to being ready to step up to the Ironman start line, confident in your preparation. How you handle the final few weeks are every bit as important as what you've accomplished over the prior months of training.

Last Peak Week

I consider the final tune-up to start four weeks out from race day. Assuming a three week taper, this puts you at the final *peak* training week. This is the time to "put a cap" on all the hard work you've done previously. During the early part of this week, plan a challenging yet achievable bike/run workout. Work hard, watch your nutrition and visualize yourself on the Ironman course. At the conclusion of this workout, you should feel tired but confident and think, "I am ready. I can do this!"

The Taper Weeks

This is a very tricky three weeks. You need to go into it convinced that you can no longer get any stronger, but can only hurt yourself. I know it's hard to accept after all that dedicated training, but you will not lose all your hard-earned fitness as you crank down your workouts. Rather, you'll be giving your body time to recover from all the hard work and to rebuild for the task at hand on Ironman day.

During the taper period, stay out of the gym. As a general guideline, start cutting the distance of your workouts down by about 30% the first week, but keep some intensity. During the second week, cut the distances down another 30-40%. Race week activity should only be to keep loose while focusing on your nutrition, fluids and sleep.

Because your workouts will be shorter during the taper, you will discover some "found" time. After so many months of using every minute of your day, you may have forgotten how to use spare time, so here are some things that you will now have time for and that will greatly contribute to success on race day.

- **Visualize:** Use some quiet time and place (I find a dark room most conducive) and "see" yourself on race day, starting with getting into the water and completing the picture as you run gracefully across the finish line, hands high in the air in celebration. Use your senses: feel the sweat, smell the air and hear the crowds cheering for you. When visualizing, you're not only telling your mind how the day will go but you can replay these thoughts during the tough spots in the actual race. It's a very powerful tool, and there's more about it in Chapter 13.

- **Set race goals:** The training is done so now you know what your capabilities are. Set individual goals for each discipline and plan how you'll manage your race to meet these goals. Then solidly commit to this plan.
- **Bike tune-up:** Get into the bike shop (or into your garage if you do it yourself). If a mechanic is doing the final check, ask him/her to go over every nut and bolt. Race day is not when you want to discover a loose bottle cage or a bent derailleur. Then do it all again at the race site if you've had to transport your bike by air. (Tip: Luggage handlers at many airports, including Kona, turn bike cases upside down to keep them from rolling off the baggage carts. Pack accordingly, then check your bike carefully after you've unpacked it.)
- **Check your spares:** If you've never had a flat and have simply packed around the same spare tubes or tires in every race for years, open them up and check them out. Make sure they haven't hardened and cracked. If you're a newbie, practice changing both tires and tubes.
- **Make checklists:** Race week is full of little chores (gear bag check-in, special needs bags on race day, etc.). Take a tip from pilots who rely on checklists before each flight. Lay out what you're going to put in your bags and make checklists. When it's time to fill your bags, simply pull out your lists and check off each item. Then you can get a sound night's sleep knowing you haven't forgotten anything.
- **Stay calm:** During the last week, there's lots of opportunity for chaos. Stay organized, get to meetings and check-ins early, walk around slowly and always carry fluid for sipping. Keep things under control, which will be easy to do because you've done the training, you have a well-tuned bike with good spares and you have checklists to work from. And don't let yourself become intimidated by others who want to convince you that they have the one and only answer to race day success. Stay calm and confident in your own race plan.

By the way — and this is a weird one — if you can't stay calm? Don't get tense about it! On race day, I guarantee that the butterflies will settle down the instant the cannon goes off and you'll be on your way to one of the best days of your life.

PART FOUR

Olympic triathlete Jennifer Gutierrez visualizing her race

Photo: Tim Carlson

PART IV — TRAINING THE MIND

Take your body where your mind wants to go.
Gatorade

13 Using Your Head – Visualization

Earlier we talked about physical preparation and looked at workouts to prepare your body to perform at its best on race day. Now let's look at the second piece of the equation: Mental Preparation.

When we watch Natascha Badmann or Peter Reid cutting through the Kona winds on their bikes and running effortlessly down Ali'i Drive, the thought that runs through all our minds is: "I want to look like that." Well, we may never be race leaders like Natascha and Peter, but there is hope of doing our own race well and looking good doing it. It's not just vanity, either. Looking good means you're keeping your form, so if you're looking good, you're doing good.

To cross the finish line in style takes a lot of dedicated, smart training, building endurance and strength along with efficient technique. Learning to fuel your body with proper nutrition and to manage pain are part of the equation as well. We read books, surf the net, buy training tools and pay coaches all in an effort to find the magic bullet on race day. But there's another very powerful training aid each of us has at our disposal that we often neglect: the mind.

Visualization

Let me start with three examples of what I consider to be great success in using the mind-body connection:

- Evander Holyfield, the four-time world heavyweight boxing champ who is currently making a comeback at 44 years of age, uses "shadow boxing" as a training technique. When I recently watched a session, he explained to me that he was going through each round of an upcoming bout— every punch, counterpunch and bob and weave that he anticipated would occur when he got in the ring with his opponent. He was playing out the match, in his mind and with his body, making it go the way he wanted it to happen. On fight night he knocked out his opponent in the second round, a little earlier than expected, but it happened just the way he'd visualized. You don't have to be a boxing fan to appreciate that.
- Heidi Musser, a blind athlete, has obvious limitations on her ability to train. She needs another person to be her eyes while swimming, biking or running and that's not always available to her. So she spends much of her training time visualizing what she's going to do on race day. To see Heidi make her way through the very tough course in the San Diego Challenged Athletes Half Ironman, you'd almost believe she'd been training every day out on the course.
- And then there's Natascha. She continues to amaze everyone with each new high-performance win. Natascha, however, is not amazed. She's "seen" it many times in her mind as she trained for the day. She's spoken about this vital part of her training that seems to result in her floating through the Kona winds with a perpetual smile and a peaceful look that tells you it's all going according to plan.

If I wasn't a believer in the mind-body connection before, these three special athletes would make a believer of me. But learning to use visualization successfully isn't always easy. Here are a few ideas that might help:

- Start small. Begin with 3-4 minutes and build up as you have success with it. This is similar to how Eastern mystics teach meditation.
- Get comfortable. Lie down in a quiet (preferably dark) place and close your eyes. If you like life with a soundtrack, use calming music as a background.
- Relax and let the tension go. Deep-breathing or progressive muscle relaxation can help.
- Empty your mind. Try to see nothing. If it helps, see a big circle and watch it get smaller and smaller until it's gone and only a blank screen remains. This is a real trick and not easily mastered. Keep working on it.
- Fill in the blank screen with a setting of your choice. See and feel all the detail.
- Put yourself in the picture. See yourself moving effortlessly, looking as graceful in your movements as that pro athlete you admire.
- If you're preparing for a specific race, put yourself on the course. Start with pre-race and work up to the point where you can stay focused while taking yourself through the entire event, anticipating potential problems, solving them and moving on. For a distance race, this will of course be compressed into a time frame over which you can maintain focus (e.g., 20-30 minutes). Let yourself truly feel the thrill and excitement as you cross the finish line looking like the first place finisher.

Visualization is a learned skill. Don't expect to be effective with it on your first try. Stop when you lose your focus and find your mind roaming. Doing it often and doing it well is what will make it an effective training tool.

You still may not cross the finish line with Peter or Natascha, but you can have your own personal record, just as you did dozens of times in your mind.

14 Workouts for Mental Preparation

When all else is equal among athletes, the one who is the strongest mentally will win the day. Even if you're not looking to the podium but are just intent on accomplishing a personal goal, your physical ability will take you partway, but it's a strong mind that will get you to the finish line. Therefore, an essential part of preparing for an Ironman is training the mind to be strong and positive on race day. Here are a few ideas for workouts that will train your head right along with your body:

Do your long workouts by yourself. We all know that having company during a long workout makes it go faster and feel less painful. But an Ironman race is an individual effort and any close company you have that day (at least on the bike) will only jeopardize you with the marshals. Learn during your long training efforts how to rely only on yourself to stay focused and positive during the bad patches.

Do your long runs on a 2-loop course and negative split the last half. This will force you to focus throughout the effort, running conservatively on the first lap at a pace that you feel confident you can beat on the second lap. It will also force you to pay attention to your form because you won't be able to accomplish this if you lose your form during the last half of the run. You'll learn to keep your head in the game, making for a stronger mind on race day.

Push the pace on the last few miles of your long ride. It's very tempting on the final stretch to spin your way home, the hard work already behind you. This is the time to refocus and push the pace, keeping your heart rate up. You'll be in pain and wanting it to be over, but isn't it better to learn to handle that feeling during training so that you'll know how to deal with it on race day?

In reading the paragraphs above, you'll notice that the word "focus" appears again and again. This is not poor writing, but rather a key word for the mental aspect of training and racing. You can let your mind disassociate (drift off and think of more pleasant things) which will help the miles pass more quickly and ease the pain, but only temporarily because it will also cause you to slow down considerably and make for a much longer race. A more productive approach is to keep your mind focused and your head in the game.

Naturally, in an Ironman race it's not possible to stay totally focused throughout the long day, and it becomes harder as the day wears on. When it's late and you're exhausted and the finish line seems to be a world away, it's easy to lose all rational thought. This brings to mind a story that, even if it's not true, should be.

Lyn Lemaire, the first woman to do Ironman, tells of one year in Kona when she was having a particularly tough go of it. It was very late out on the dark lava fields and she was simply trying to put one foot in front of the other. Out of the darkness, she saw the image of a man holding an ice cold, frothy mug of beer in his hand. "All you have to do is quit," he softly said as he held the beer up to her face. Lynn swears that it was the devil talking to her. As I said, it's easy to lose all rational thought.

I recommend having a plan that you can put into place when you hit a bad patch and feel you need a little help staying focused, which you're guaranteed to experience during an Ironman race. One idea you can try is to assess your running form – head up, shoulders relaxed, arms swinging comfortably, etc. Along with this, count your turnover. This is a simple task until about mile 18 of an Ironman run. It will require all your mental capacity, which requires focus – the ultimate goal.

Another trick is to have something prepared to run through your head. Some call it a mantra, others call it talking to yourself. Whatever you choose to call it, think about it ahead of time rather than expecting to be creative at that point. Make it meaningful to you, something that will motivate or inspire you or maybe even make you chuckle.

One that I've used as motivation during rough patches is to remind myself that there's no place else I'd rather be at the moment. I then smile when I think: *Except, of course, at the finish line.*

To paraphrase the always entertaining sports legend Yogi Berra: An Ironman race is 50% physical; the other 80% is mental. So don't neglect giving your mind a workout right along with your body during all those long training hours.

> *Champions are made when nobody is watching.*
> *Me*

Many-time Ironman age group world champion Joe Bonness

Photo: Erick Kellar/Naples Daily News

15 The Ironman Run: It's a Mind Game

The difference between a pure marathon and an Ironman marathon
is that the Ironman marathon is harder.
Everybody

Not a very profound statement. It's fairly obvious, to even a novice, that running on very tired legs for that distance will hurt and is going to require a full dose of pain management. What may not be so obvious is that it will also be extremely hard mentally. If you have demons (and who among us doesn't at some time?), an Ironman run is a perfect playground for them. You may have doubts passing through your mind that run along these lines: "This is too hard"; "I have to walk"; "I will never make it to the finish line"; "I don't know what I was thinking"; "Never again," etc. This type of negative thinking can make the run seem even longer and harder than it actually is.

But the truth of the matter is this: You *can* do it. You can manage the pain and the demons if you're prepared for both. Putting in the training miles with long, back-to-back workouts will teach you to anticipate and manage the pain but going into the event with a mental game plan is something that is often overlooked. So let's take a look at some ideas for handling the mental part of an Ironman marathon.

Race Day

With winds blasting and heat building every passing hour, the bike leg seems to go on interminably, making it impossible to keep that nagging little thought out of your mind – "How am I going to make these tired legs run a marathon?" Regardless of how many long-distance rides you've done in training, this one feels longer and harder. As you approach T2, you do it with very mixed emotions. You're so glad to be done with the 112 miles but leery about the 26.2 mile task ahead. You've seen the pros race through transition, hardly missing a beat, and hope to look that relaxed yourself. But instead your legs feel like lead,

you're hobbling like an old man and *running* to the changing tent is out of the question. You're just hoping you can make it into the tent with your painfully unsteady walk. And thus begins the Ironman marathon.

A Mile at a Time

With the first step onto the course, the thought of 4 hours, 26 miles, 3 loops, etc. is enough to make even the strongest among us fall apart. But the thought of one mile seems less daunting at this point. So make that your goal: one mile at a time. Never let yourself look beyond the next mile. This is a mind game, but the entire marathon is a mind game and this one can be quite effective.

A Port in the Storm

The aid stations, fortunately for the above-mentioned strategy, are at every mile along the course. These not only become the goal points for your one-mile runs, but someone is always waiting for you there. They'll welcome you, offer you food and drink, help you with simple medical issues, provide porta-johns and generally just be a beacon in the night. Make sure you don't leave there without getting the nutrition you need. (Try the chicken broth — it's to die for!) And take the opportunity to interact, however briefly, with the volunteers. You'd be surprised at the energy you can draw from them.

Use the Crowd

Most Ironman run courses are designed to be spectator friendly, which also makes them racer friendly. Seeing friends, family and total strangers who are clapping, yelling and offering support can boost your spirits and make you run a little taller (read: faster). I've found that you get more from the crowds when you smile and thank them for their encouraging words. And when someone asks you "How're you feeling?" don't tell them the truth. Answer "Great!" and you might find you actually believe it, if only for a few minutes.

Never Give In

Every Ironman racer, at some point in the run, is tempted to give up the race plan and simply make it to the finish line. While it's true that completing the 140.6 miles is a major accomplishment, you probably went into the day with a race plan – times you thought you were

Kevin Moats, whose ability to stay focused for long periods has resulted in a string of incredible Ironman performances

trained for. But, no matter how well trained you are, the difficulty of an Ironman marathon can easily become overwhelming and cause you to feel that you're not able to do what you originally thought. This is the time to remember: *Whether you believe you can or whether you believe you can't, you're always right.*

So suck it up and believe you can.

No matter how many Ironman races you do, the run will always be a challenge like no other. But then, the accomplishment of completing an Ironman is like no other as well. So, to my way of thinking, it's a challenge well worth taking on. Go to the start line with a strong mind as well as a strong body and enjoy your achievement.

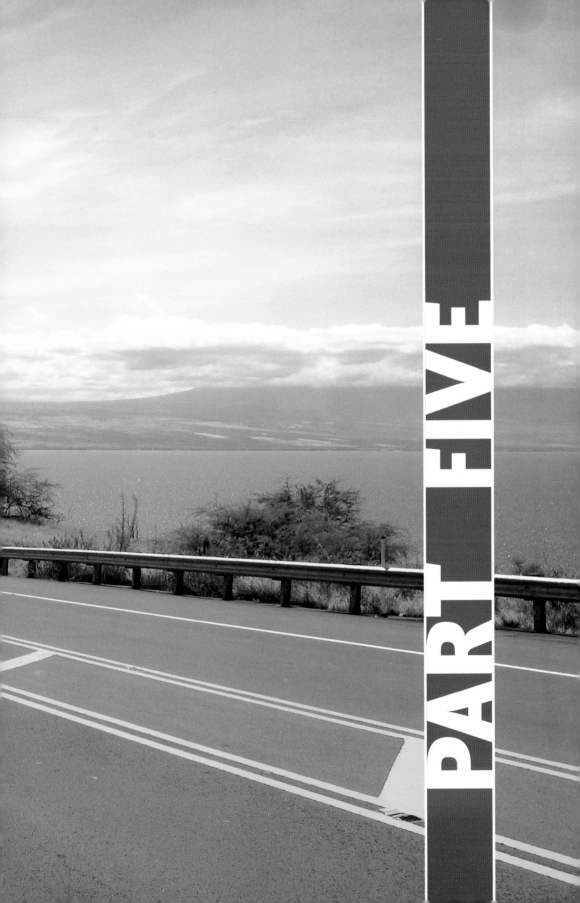

PART FIVE

Nick Martin training for his first Kona Ironman

Photo: Lee Gruenfeld

PART V — CHECKING PROGRESS

The more I practice, the luckier I get.
Gary Player

16 Is Your Training Program Working for You?

Once your season is in full swing, you'll want to have a method for evaluating how your program is working for you. Racing your goal event will certainly test how successful your training has been, but by then it's too late. You need ways to take stock of things along the way and make any necessary modifications well in advance of race day.

Before talking about how to measure progress, it's important to remember that an Ironman race requires you not only to go the distance but to be strong and efficient throughout all three disciplines, which will translate into speed. We only have a finite amount of energy, and success on Ironman day depends on the effective allocation of that energy over the three legs. Therefore, the Ironman training goal is a two-fold one:

1 To increase the amount of energy you have to work with on race day (*Fitness*)
2 To learn how to dole out that energy so you remain strong throughout the entire day (*Efficiency*)

Fitness is fairly objective and not unlike that of a pure biker, swimmer or runner. *Efficiency* is a key factor in endurance events. Both should be taken into account when measuring your progress. The bottom line is that you're looking for an increase in your overall speed while maintaining the same or a lower heart rate, which means you're increasing your efficiency over the distance.

A fast finishing time in an Ironman will be the result of keeping your form and technique through to the finish line. Shouldn't we, then, measure how we are improving in this regard rather than seeking to run a faster 440 at the track, swim a quicker 100 in the pool or hammer with the "big boys" on the bike? There is most certainly a place for these kinds of workouts, but not as a measurement tool for assessing your progress towards the ultimate goal, which is a long distance race.

Here are some ideas for measuring your Ironman training progress:

Fitness

The easiest way to assess progress is using time trials. Ideally, you want the same environment and conditions each time you test. With the swim, that's fairly easy as most pools, for our purposes, are interchangeable. A track or a treadmill is the most controlled environment for a running test and a trainer eliminates the elements as a factor during the bike test.

Because you're training for distance, the time trials in each discipline should not be short bursts of speed but rather an effort that lets you build up and maintain your speed, such as a 1000 yard swim, a 15-20 mile ride and a 30-40 minute run. The results of these time trials should be measured in three ways:

- Overall time — you want it lower than the last time you tested
- Maximum heart rate required for the effort — you want to lower that, too
- Reduction of heart rate in the sixty seconds following the effort — you want this to happen faster

Efficiency

In the pool, swim 1000 yards with the objective of keeping the same stroke count through to the finish. If you lose the ability to keep it constant, note the distance and stop. The next time try to increase the distance over which you're able to maintain the same stroke count. Your improvement will show in faster times over longer distances without an increase in your stroke count, which means you're a more efficient swimmer. (If you are able to keep a constant stroke count throughout the entire 1000 yards, your check of progress is simply lower times for the distance.)

On the bike, the goal is to handle the same work load with a lower heart rate. Find a long distance route that has a couple of short, steep hills. After you top a hill and have a raised heart rate from the climbing effort, note your heart rate, then note it again after sixty seconds of lesser effort. Heart rate recovery is an excellent measurement of both fitness and efficiency. Overall improvement will show in riding similar or faster times over the same course with both a lower heart rate throughout and a faster reduction in heart rate following bouts of harder effort.

The goal for your run is to keep your leg turnover quick and constant which can happen only if you're running with good technique: standing tall, shoulders and arms relaxed. This is not too difficult to maintain while running a mile, but it's very difficult as the run goes into the second and third hour. As mentioned in a previous chapter, find a course where you can break the distance into two laps. Strive for a negative split, which will require you to run the first lap conservatively and keep good form and technique in the second lap. If your running program is working, the negative split will become easier and more natural.

Do these tests every 4-5 weeks. As with all testing, don't make major changes to your plan if there's not improvement each time. Remember, life happens and some days we're just not as strong as other days. But if you find there's no improvement over a couple of measurement tests, perhaps it's time to reevaluate your program and make some changes. Also, the amount of improvement to expect is directly related to your experience as an athlete and can be affected by your age. If you've been training and racing well for years, you should expect smaller levels of improvement than someone who is just beginning, and if you're moving into your upper years, you're probably kidding yourself if you expect to perform as you did when you were thirty. (Or fifty!)

It has been my experience that the very act of testing and continual evaluation keeps one progressing forward. Just keep in mind that pure speed is to be enjoyed but shouldn't be considered the sole predictor of Ironman success. It's the ability to continue strong through to the finish line that will make the day a great one.

PART SIX

Elizabeth Farnan putting aside training on a Kona afternoon

Photo: Lee Gruenfeld

PART VI —
REST: THE KEY INGREDIENT

On the seventh day, I rested.
God

17 Work + Recovery = Peak Performance

A strong body obeys; a weak body commands.
Andre Agassi

Triathletes spend hours and hours swimming, biking, running and working in the gym hoping to train their bodies for peak performance on race day. While this work is one half of the equation, the other half, recovery, is of equal importance and should be a vital part of any athlete's training program. Bodybuilders have known this since the beginning of the sport, but other kinds of athletes sometimes take more convincing.

Recovery takes several forms:

Recovery During Workouts
When doing interval work in any discipline, the objective is to follow the hard effort with recovery before starting the next work effort. If your goal is speed, the effort will be close to all out and the recovery should be long enough to get completely rested before starting the next hard effort. If endurance is what you're working on, the efforts are less intense (more sustainable) and the recovery period is shorter so that you start the next effort without being fully recovered, thereby building endurance. Short or long, proper recovery is the key to getting the maximum benefit from each work effort.

Recovery Between Workouts
As many of us do during July, I watch the Tour de France and admire the biking skills of these guys. But another thing I've noticed is how quickly they go from crossing the finish line to getting inside the team trailer. Now, I realize there's an element of avoiding the press to this, but the major goal is to begin the recovery process as quickly as possible, knowing as they do that they'll be hard at it again in less than 18 hours.

After a hard workout day, we mere mortals have the very same issue. We have a training plan that calls for another hard workout day in less than 18 hours. Seems like we should take a cue from these pros and get our recovery started immediately after the workout. Although we don't have a team of people to take care of our every need as the Tour boys do, here are some thoughts on overnight recovery:

- Food and drink are of paramount importance, so start eating and drinking quickly. The body will work most efficiently in taking in the nutrients and using them for rebuilding during the first 60-90 minutes after your workout. Use that window to full advantage.

- Ice is a miracle healer. After a hard workout, your leg muscles are loaded with micro-tears. During your downtime, these small tears will heal, and that's what makes your legs stronger. Ice will help this process along. Sitting in an ice bath is a wonderful way to ice your entire lower body, although many athletes feel this therapy is simply too onerous. It becomes less so if you put on a sweatshirt and take some good compelling reading material with you. Ten minutes of this torture is all you need to improve your recovery.

- Make sure your meals include some protein, the building blocks for your recovery. Throw some chicken, fish, tuna or turkey into a pasta or a rice stir-fry with some veggies added, et voila! You have the perfect recovery meal.

- Get your legs up. Lying on the floor and putting them up against the wall or up on the bed is a great method for this, but sitting in a recliner also works well and is a bit more civilized. While you're elevating your legs, do some gentle stretching and self-massage as well.

- If it's available to you, take advantage of a good massage. Make sure it's a therapist who is sports-oriented and understands your recovery goals.

- Napping is also a good recovery tool. All you need is 10 minutes of sleep for it to be beneficial.

- If your job takes you from the workout directly to your office, a little creativity may be required. Have your food and drink planned so you can take it to your desk with you. An ice bath, even if you're truly committed to the torture method, may not be in the cards, but you can fill a couple of ice packs and sit on those for 20 minutes for the hips and glutes or wrap them around your sore knees if that's a vulnerable area for you. Your work situation may not be conducive to lying on the floor to get your legs up, but you can get some benefit from self-massage and stretching.

All these recovery strategies are also appropriate if your recovery is between "two-a-day" workouts rather than overnight. Start your recovery process as soon as you finish the morning workout, which will prepare you for the evening workout.

Pre-emptive or Forced Recovery

There are times when downtime is forced on us, either to prevent injury or illness or after it's occurred. In either case, recovery time is critical to long-term good performance. The prescription for this is dependent on your specific circumstances, but a general guideline is to get a definitive diagnosis from a sports doc as soon as possible and understand that denial won't solve the problem. Then get to work on your recovery.

Planned work sprinkled with the proper doses of recovery at the appropriate times will give you the performance you've been dreaming of.

PART SEVEN

Photo: Lee-Gue...

PART VII
— SOMETIMES IT HURTS

Setbacks pave the way for comebacks.
Evander Holyfield

18 Injuries Happen

An injury, such as a sprained ankle from running or a broken collar bone suffered in a bike crash, can occur at any time, even while following the healthiest training program. However, some athletes actually invite trouble when they start to feel that more is better and fall into the overtraining trap. That can lead to injuries like pulled muscles and stress fractures.

Regardless of how it happened, you're going to find yourself trying to get back into the game as quickly as possible. To do that you're going to need an effective approach to healing both mentally and physically. The physical side is dependent on the injury and I don't have much to add to what's already known about that. As for the mental side of healing, it's really all about two things: *patience* and *handling downtime productively.*

Your first and hardest challenge is to reconcile yourself to the situation. Fighting it simply delays the healing process and, if in your denial you continue to work the injury, you're risking further and potentially more serious damage. The sooner you come to grips with it, the sooner the body can devote all its energy to the healing process. Use the first 24 hours to feel sorry for yourself and then face facts and get on with it. Here are some ideas for doing that:

- Take some time away from the activity that caused the problem. Allow yourself plenty of time rather than testing the injury every day or setting a hard and fast timetable for returning to full training. Replace training time with other activities that you enjoy and which will keep you active.

- Happiness is having something to look forward to, even if it's 12-18 months away. Set a new race goal, but be realistic and take into account the severity of the injury. In some cases, the immediate goal is recovery and the race goal becomes a next year goal. Give yourself plenty of time; rushing the comeback is a recipe for further injury and missing your race goal.

- Refocus on activities that you tend to neglect when training full-time. Stay productive. Set new goals in non-physical areas, but make them short-term enough so that you can accomplish them before training starts up again.

- Get involved with something where you can work with other people, helping them in some way. There's no better way to get your mind off yourself and your troubles than to get involved with people or projects where your full attention is required.

- Keep structure in your life. A triathlete is, by necessity, a creature of habit. We're used to getting started early, having a plan for the day, meeting time schedules for the pool and group rides, etc. When we're forced into downtime, the first thing we're faced with is no structure and lots of extra time. It's very easy to let depression take over, which is the beginning of a downward spiral. Try to continue your normal schedule. Get up with the alarm and start your day. But do it by taking time to read the newspaper rather than rushing off to the pool. Use your extra time to accomplish some of those things that have been on the back-burner for years – the ones that don't require using the injured parts.

- Maintain fitness with workouts that use uninjured parts of your body. Joan Benoit, the first woman Olympic marathon gold medalist, had knee surgery 17 days before the Olympic trials in 1984. One day after the procedure she was cycling with her arms while lying in bed. If you're nursing a cranky hamstring, swim with pull buoys, which will protect your hamstring while working your upper body. If you've hurt your shoulder or bruised some ribs, do some water-running or lower-body weight work or spin on your trainer. These kinds of activities may not keep your fitness level where it was, but they can get close and will also go a long way towards keeping you positive which, in turn, will accelerate the healing process.

- Don't let your healthy diet fall apart. Continued good nutrition will help hasten the physical healing and will keep you feeling good, contributing to your mental well-being. When you find yourself picking up extra weight, the most common reaction is eating while you complain about your body changing shape. This won't take you in the right direction.

- Don't be afraid to let others help you. Triathletes who are used to being strong and vital oftentimes feel very vulnerable when taken down by injury. It's a difficult thing to accept that the race season continues as you watch from the sidelines. This is a time to let others help you. Many have been where you are and have found their way back. Let them guide you.

In our chosen sport, injury is a fact of life. Some injuries can be avoided by smart training but others simply can't. Be compassionate and understanding when it happens to someone else, knowing that it will happen to you at some point. And when it does, accept it, fix it and get back in the game.

PART EIGHT

Photo: Tim Carlson

PART VIII — RACE DAY

There are no big moments you can reach unless you've a pile of smaller
moments to stand on.
Lillian Hellman

19 Critical Success Factors for a Great Ironman

Ironman is a day of *crisis management*. But don't let that scare you because you can be prepared. That preparation will allow you to avoid a potential crisis or, if it should happen, to handle it and move on.

Training and racing successfully can appear complicated. We have a wide variety of publications dedicated to providing tips on how to do it. There are plenty of coaches available to guide the process, and advice from someone who's just completed his or her first Ironman is usually plentiful. From my experience over the years, I've tried to uncomplicate it just a bit and have narrowed it down to the following six Critical Success Factors for a great Ironman venture. In no particular order of importance:

- **If you eat and drink enough, you can do anything.**

    Although the drop-out rate in an Ironman is extremely low (You worked too hard to get there and are not about to quit), those who do get forced out often blame it on their nutrition — didn't get enough or couldn't keep it down. You must have a nutrition plan and execute it just as judiciously as you manage your pace. Eat early and often, keeping the fuel tanks topped off. It takes training to get your belly used to this so that's when you experiment to find the right fuel and teach your gut to handle the level of intake that's going to be required on race day.

    What you eat is a very individual matter. A case in point is veteran Ironman Sue Osborn, who held the F30-34 record in Kona for a whopping thirteen years. The night before the race, she'd go to Wendy's for a big, greasy cheeseburger which she put in her special needs bag the following morning. At the halfway point on the bike, she'd eat her cheeseburger and fly through the rest of the race. Her rationale was simple: On her long training rides, there was a

Wendy's at the halfway point. She got used to scarfing down a cheeseburger in training, so that's what she did - quite successfully - on race day.

I'm not advocating following Sue's choice of nutrition, but you can hardly refute the wisdom of using by race day what worked for you in training.

- **Efficiency Will Save the Day**

You have a very long day ahead of you and a finite amount of energy to power you through it. The key to avoiding a crisis is to dole out your energy very carefully, saving some for the end when it's most needed. What will allow you to do that is focusing on being efficient, and you'll need to work on this during training so that it's "burned in" by race day.

Maintaining good technique is the surest way to use energy efficiently, so you need to continually focus on that. However, few of us are able to maintain that level of concentration for the duration of an Ironman or even a long training session. But we can learn to focus frequently for shorter periods.

Swim: long strokes, head down, stretch and roll
Bike: smooth pedal turnover, steady cadence, relaxed upper body
Run: chin up; shoulders down; relaxed swing of arms at your sides rather than crossing the body; relaxed fists; quick, light steps; cadence of around 90

Every so often (you'll learn to do it automatically through training) go through your checklist. Doing this throughout the long day should help you to keep good technique and thereby use the least amount of energy.

- **Mental Toughness**

For most people an Ironman race is half physical and half mental, but from about mile 18 of the run to the finish, it's 100% mental for everyone. Therefore, doesn't it make sense that mental toughness training and a race day mental strategy be part of the plan? In training, doing your long bike and run workouts solo will make you stronger mentally. On race day, you're on your own when it comes to getting through the bad patches and staying positive. Better to make this something you've experienced and managed in training rather than dealing with it for the first time on race day. While out there training on your own, if you have the choice of a headwind or tailwind, flat or hilly, easy or tough, backing off when it gets hard or powering through it, always make the decision for the tougher alternative. You'll get a better physical workout and you'll come home mentally stronger.

On race day, staying in the moment is a good strategy. Looking at the long journey ahead when you stand at the water's edge is enough to intimidate even the toughest athlete. Look only at where you are and what you have to do right now. You will have, pre-race, broken down the bike and run courses into smaller, more manageable pieces, which makes them easier. Go to work on the immediate task at hand and when you finish, regardless of how fast or slow you covered it, put it behind you and move on, thinking only of where you are and what you have to do to get through the next piece.

- **Do the Race You're Prepared For**

By the time race day comes around, you'll know from your training what you're prepared to do and how you'll do it. The only unknown should be the conditions, and part of your race day planning should be to play through in your mind the adjustments you'll make if weather becomes an issue.

Set three goals (swim, bike, run) based on your training, experience, the course and expected conditions. Work on these goals as three separate events, never adjusting one because of what's occurred in the previous event. Make race day just another long training day — you've done it dozens of times before. This is a key approach in avoiding a race day crisis.

- **It's All About the Run**

  An Ironman race includes three disciplines and it's not over until you accomplish the 26.2 mile marathon. No awards are given for having a swim or bike personal record on that day. And having a good run starts during the 114.4 miles in the water and on the bike, before you put on your running shoes. Pace yourself and execute a good nutrition plan in preparation for the run and, instead of finding yourself explaining why your run time exceeded your bike time, you'll be accepting hearty congratulations on a great Ironman race.

- **Believe You Can Do It – With All Your Heart**

  When preparing for our first Ironman, each of us has said, aloud or to ourselves, "I know I can swim 2.4 miles and bike 112 miles and run 26.2 miles. But can I do all three together?" If you've had a well-designed training program, the answer is: Yes, you can. A good training program is designed to get you to the finish line and carries with it a subtle but important message: if you can do the training, you can do the race. So if you do the training, be confident that you can do the race.

  As I said before, whether you believe you can or whether you believe you can't...you're always right.

20 Breaking It Down

Triathletes obviously think of their races as the three disciplines (swim/bike/run) plus the two transitions (T1 and T2). That's fine for shorter distant races. Ironman, however, is a very different animal and requires a different perspective. A better strategy is to break the "King of Triathlons" down a little finer than that, because there are several points in the race that can be critical to our success and yet we tend to just lump them in with the swim, bike and run.

Specifically, I'm referring to:

A   the last few minutes of the swim (preparing for the bike)
B   the first few minutes of the bike
C   the last few minutes of the bike (preparing for the run)
D   the first few minutes of the run

We all know that you need to get settled into the bike and the run quickly. But what is the best way to go about that? By breaking it down, as follows:

A. The last few minutes of the swim

Although it's generally good advice to "stay in the moment," I contend that, shortly before the end of the swim, your time would be well spent starting the mental changeover from being a swimmer to becoming a cyclist.

If you've been kicking big, slow it down. Let those large muscles rest a bit with a two-beat kick. Start visualizing the transition and see yourself — in detail — going through the motions of getting out of the water, shedding the swim gear and donning bike gear.

In this visualization, make sure to see yourself as *calm*. This will not only get you mentally prepared for a quick and efficient T1 but will keep you on an even keel when you get caught in the frenzy that begins in the finishing chute of the swim.

B. The first few minutes of the bike

The important thought to carry out of T1 is that no one's race is won or lost in the first five minutes of the bike leg, regardless of what that guy hammering out of transition thinks. 112 miles makes for a long time in the saddle whether you're a pro or a first-timer. So the objective is to settle into an efficient pedal stroke and, as quickly as possible, bring your heart rate down to the zone in which you'll spend the day. As soon as you're there, and no sooner, go ahead and top off the fuel tanks, making up for what you've lost during the swim.

You'll find yourself calm, well-fed and riding efficiently. Relax onto the aerobars and you've set yourself up for a rock solid second leg of your Ironman.

C. The last few minutes of the bike

When we see our computers turn over to Mile 105, 106..., there's not a one of us who isn't ready, mentally and physically, to be done with the bike. If this were a Saturday ride with the group, we'd be all set to roll into a Starbucks, cozy up to a double latte and brag about hammering the big hills as we rest our trashed legs.

But this is no Saturday ride with the guys and you've got a marathon to run. So when you get close to T2, start preparing. Stop eating and drinking for those last few miles. You don't want any Gatorade sloshing around in your belly as you start running and you'll start refueling again as soon as you get settled into the run. It's time to get the trashed legs ready for their next task, so ratchet it down a notch and spin, giving your legs some much-needed relief. Stand and stretch out your back and your glutes. Your body has been in the aero or sitting position for many, many hours, so wake it up with as much moving around as is reasonable considering you're still on two wheels.

If you watch your competition zoom on ahead to T2 as you spin and stretch, don't worry. Sticking to your preparation plan will serve you very well and they'll wish they'd followed suit as you pass them in Mile Two of the run looking strong and steady.

D. The first few minutes of the run

Even with all that brick training, your legs will likely still feel like bricks. But *because* of all that brick training, you know that you can get settled in and run well.

That first mile is all mind game. The body wants more time to get going while the mind wants it to start running well *right now*. Relax, and try to see yourself running like a pro. Don't let yourself think about the 26.2 miles ahead. Your short term goal is getting to the first mile marker, as though it were a separate stage of the race, and being in the groove when you reach it. That's also where the crowds usually are. Use them. Run well as they cheer you on.

Incorporate these suggestions into your overall game plan and I believe you'll be setting yourself up for a breakthrough race.

21 Something for Nothing

When we have a great race, it's payback for all the hard training that's been put in the bank. But a triathlete has one potential advantage that is unique in the sporting world, a part of our event where we can buy time for free — no anaerobic training required —and that's in the transitions.

It's easy to overlook T1 and T2 as places to buy time. Instead, we look at them as a necessary few minutes that you add in when you're setting your race goal. However, the first time the television cameras caught Paula Newby-Fraser shooting past the T1 tent in Kona, going straight from the water to her bike and leaving her competition staring in wonder, people started looking at transitions a little differently.

Regretfully, none of us is Paula, but there are things that we mere mortals can do that cost nothing and can speed things along. As an Ironman, look at your race as three separate events and your transitions as time to prepare yourself for the last two.

Although the following ideas are generally to make your transitions as fast as possible, there are two overall guidelines I'll offer that may add a few seconds but will pay back over the long haul:
1 Get into comfortable clothes to make it easier to ride and run your best.
2 Stay calm during the transitions so you make fewer mistakes.

T1 (Swim to Bike)
• First, know the transition: Do you have a long run? Is the ground rocky and would shoes make it easier? Will there be wetsuit "strippers" and where will they be? Where do you pick up your gear bag? Prior to race day, take a walking tour of the trip from the water, through the transition and then to your bike, making sure you understand each step of the way.
• Wear as much as you can in the water, under your "FastSkin" or your wetsuit: biking shorts, singlet, number belt.
• If there are volunteers, let them help you. They are calmer and frequently have a lot more experience than you do, so let them do their job. They'll get you out the door quickly and won't let you

forget anything. (Or at least, anything conventional. They have no way to know what special things you plan to do or take.)

- Stage whatever you can on the bike — helmet, shoes, food. In some races, age group athletes are not allowed to leave biking shoes on their bike. In that case, carry your shoes while you run to the bike and put them on before mounting, unless the ground is unsuitable for running barefoot.
- If you are the fair skin type, take the few seconds to let a volunteer smear some SPF on your back. Eight or nine hours later, you'll be glad you did...or very sorry you didn't.

T2 (Bike to Run)

This transition is a little less complicated, although you'll be much more tired and perhaps a bit stiff and wobbly. Again, let the volunteers guide you through it. Be sure when you take your walking tour from the water through T1 that you also examine where you come in from the bike course, the exact location of your gear bag and how you get in and out of T2. Practice what you'll need to do in T2 and you can have a very quick changeover, leaving your competition wondering where you went.

Take off your shoes and helmet as soon as you pass off your bike to a volunteer. (But do not remove your helmet until the bike has left your hands, if you hope to continue your race.) Grab your gear bag (you know exactly where it is); put on your socks and shoes using lace locks of some sort; grab your food and your hat and start running out of transition. You can put your food away and your hat on while you're getting onto the run course. If you haven't been wearing your number belt on the bike, carry it along with your hat and put it on as you're running. You'll be happy to discover you've covered quite some distance just "getting dressed."

Here are some more ideas for setting yourself up for fast transitions and a great race:

- If you wear socks on the bike, put a second pair in your T2 bag. If you've been peeing on the bike (which you should be), you'll be grateful for a change of socks before starting the run.
- Volunteers will turn your bags upside down and empty them. If you have your bike shoes in your bag, you don't want the cleats to

break your fragile sunglasses. You can prevent this by putting your sunglasses in a hard case or firmly inside one of the shoes.

- If you have fair skin, put SPF on the night before. Get body marked in the morning (the overnight SPF won't interfere with that) and then put on another layer before the start.
- If appropriate, practice getting out of your wetsuit using a stripper. It can be a split-second process if done right and an embarrassingly clumsy and prolonged one if not.
- To assure yourself of calm during the gear bag packing process, make a checklist. Then simply use the list and relax in the knowledge that you've not forgotten anything.
- Visualize your transitions just as you visualize other parts of your race day. Know exactly what you're going to do and how it's going to unfold.

Take advantage of the two times during race day that don't depend on long hours of training. Be smooth and calm and you'll have fewer minutes to add when trying to meet your race goals.

WATER

Gatorade

FOOD

19 mi.

PART NINE

Photo: Lee Gruenfeld

PART IX – THE OFF-SEASON

To everything, there is a season.
Ecclesiastes

22 Ironman Recovery

You've done it!
You prepared for it for months, perhaps years, and now you've experienced that high of crossing the finish line of an Ironman. You discovered the heady feeling that comes with this accomplishment and believe that, having done it, you can do practically anything...and you're right. You're a hero to your spouse, kids and neighbors. Your fellow workers throw you a congratulations party when you return to the office.

So now what?

The first few days after an Ironman race, you'll feel sore. Walking up and down stairs is not the simple task it used to be but when that issue goes away in a few days, it's a mistake to think that you're recovered. You're not. This is the time to recall all the hard work you put your body through in preparation for the race and understand that it now needs some time to repair and recover fully. However, both your body and mind have gotten used to a certain level of work, so giving up exercise completely is counterproductive in this recovery effort.

A very common malady at this point is the Post-Ironman Blues. For months, you've had a goal. Every minute of your busy life had a purpose, a very specific direction, and suddenly that's all behind you, which can be a tremendous letdown, not dissimilar to post-partum depression. The response to this usually comes in one of two forms:

1   You can't get yourself out of bed in the morning. After all, it doesn't matter if you miss that swim workout now. Or...

2   You sign up for a century bike ride and a marathon two weeks away. After all, you can do anything, remember?

Both of these responses will eventually take you where you don't want to be.

The "I Don't Have to Do It Anymore" Syndrome
If you find yourself eating more doughnuts than PowerBars and getting out of bed just in time to meet the Saturday riders for lunch, it's time to set another goal for yourself. This goal need not be a swim/bike/run goal. The purpose of setting this new goal is to get yourself redirected and focused again rather than on to a new level of fitness. This is an excellent time to do some of those things that Ironman training didn't allow for. Contrary to the philosophy by which you've lived during the past few months, you won't lose all your fitness if you don't swim, bike or run for a few weeks. Rather it will ensure that you'll return to triathlon training with renewed vigor.

The "I Am Superman" Syndrome

Once the soreness abates, it's very easy to slip back into your regular training routine, but this can adversely affect what you have planned in the months ahead.

If your Ironman race was a mid-season race and you have another Ironman in your near future, it's imperative that you manage your recovery well. In the final weeks before your race, you followed some sort of taper, cutting down the duration while keeping up the intensity of your work efforts. Each week you probably cut back more until race week when your emphasis was on resting, with very short workouts only to keep loose. A good way to recover after the race is to "reverse taper": The first week emphasize rest, keeping stretched and loose, and each week increase the duration of your workouts slightly for the same number of weeks that you tapered.

If your race was an end-of-your-season event, you have a little more latitude in your recovery routine. If the group is doing a century and you don't want to be left out, go for it, but be aware that you may not be at your best so don't plan to hammer with the leaders. Remember: you're an Ironman now and don't have anything left to prove!

If you hope to be in the Ironman game for the long haul, recovery is as important a part of your training as the long ride or the transition run. Manage it well and the payback will be huge.

23 What to Do When There's Nothing to Do

Actually, there's plenty to do.

Whether you raced Kona in October or Lake Placid in July, the season is complete, your goals accomplished and, now, we Type A's face a new challenge — the Off-Season. The casual observer might expect a triathlete to relish time off with no pressure of a pending race schedule. However, that is frequently not the case and, in fact, some of us feel adrift during the winter months.

This is not the time to lose focus. What you do over the next few months can have a dramatic effect on the success of next season.

In the cooler climates, it's very tempting to hibernate over the winter months, assuming that the layer you add around the middle will quickly disappear when it's time to get serious again. In the warmer climates the risk runs more along the lines of "more of the same" — swimming, biking and running, long hard hammer sessions with the group. Neither of these approaches to the off-season is an ideal setup for a great upcoming season.

One sure thing about triathletes is that we function best when we have specific goals. So, even though most of us won't have specific race goals during the winter months, that doesn't preclude us from setting other, short-term goals for those months.

Here are some ideas for how to handle the winter blahs:

• This is the time when you can afford to spend plenty of quality time in the gym doing weight work. Unless your goal is a body building contest, you don't want to bulk up, but you can do some good work on biking-specific muscles, work that will pay huge dividends when you get back in the saddle.

- Each of us has at least one of the three disciplines in which we are not as competitive as we'd like. (You don't need to label this a "weakness.") It's a lot of fun to do the things we're really good at, but it's a lot more productive to spend time where we are not as strong. Without an upcoming race, you should feel more freedom to spend time doing drills, working on form and making changes that might slow you down temporarily but will have your competitors scrambling next season. (Tiger Woods took out an entire year to change his swing after winning his first Master's Tournament. I rest my case.)

- This downtime is also the perfect opportunity to give yourself a break from regularly scheduled swim/bike/run activities. Go a little nuts and do something different. Take that driven personality and climb a mountain or ski some moguls. My personal activity guideline for Nov-Dec is to do whatever I feel like doing and nothing that I feel I must do...although I hope that I feel like working on that discipline that needs work.

- It's worth noting that, with the growing popularity of the sport, Ironman races fill up very quickly, so this is also the time to plan your race schedule and get yourself officially entered. Selecting your target race(s) is a very personal business. If Kona is your Holy Grail, you'll want to make all your big races qualifiers. (You might also want to enter the lottery.) If a different Ironman race is your goal, try to find an earlier Half Ironman/70.3 to use as a training race. If your goal race is an early season Ironman (e.g. Arizona or New Zealand), you might need to kick your training program into gear a little earlier and compete without the benefit of a training race prior to your goal race. In this case, you can simulate a training race with a well planned, 3-event training day.

Base Building

Having had a couple of month's break from the rigors of regular training, you should be excited about the upcoming season and your body should have had time to repair any nagging little reminders of last season.

Base building is a necessary phase for every athlete as he/she moves into the season. The amount of base building you'll need depends upon your athletic and competitive background and your season race goals, but need it you will. Going from zero to warp speed overnight is not recommended if a successful season is what you have in mind. Build your base carefully as it's the foundation — the base — for all the training that will follow. (Read more about this in Chapter 7.)

From this point, your training plan is determined by your race schedule. If you've used the off-season to your advantage and have been disciplined during your base building, you're well on your way to another great season.

EPILOGUE —
A View from the Race Course

If you don't play to win, why keep score?
Vernon Law

Photo: John Segesta

24 Kona Memories

If you've ever entered a triathlon or even if you've only happened upon the television show of Ironman, you no doubt have a sense that Kailua-Kona, Hawai'i, and the race that plays out in that locale, are something pretty special, even magical. It draws the best in the business, amateur and professional, from all over the world, and the juxtaposed vision of the beauty of paradise and 2000 strong, fit athletes struggling mightily is mesmerizing. Somehow you know that this is the place to be in October if you are a triathlete, a wannabe or even just someone who appreciates the guts and glory that is the Super Bowl of endurance sport.

I've been lucky enough to race in Kona many times and I have memories of those years that form a clear picture of why it's so special and why so many of us are pulled back to the island every year. For those of you who have been there, you may share some of my memories and will surely have some special moments of your own. If you've not yet had the privilege of racing in Kona, keep working on getting there. It's one of those wonderful and rare experiences in life that actually lives up to the hype.

Some of my moments:
• The Kona coast comes into view as the plane approaches the airport. With every foot of altitude we lose, the ocean becomes bluer and details on the tiny road, which is the bike course, become clearer. I realize that I'm looking at what will be my "playground" for the next few days and my heart rate climbs a few beats.

• The perspective changes as the plane lands, the doors open and I'm hit with the moist Kona winds. The warm air, laced with the unique tropical smell of Hawai'i, gives me the cocoon-like sensation that I'm home again. The "Welcome to Kona" sign confirms that I belong here.

• In the early days of racing in Kona, we used to stay at the King Kam Hotel, right at the start/finish area. On race morning, I felt like I

2006 Ironman winner Michellie Jones

Photo: Lee Gruenfeld

I will never, ever, ever do an Ironman.
Michellie Jones, in 2003

gained strength for the day ahead as I bonded silently with my fellow racers at the hotel. At 4:00 a.m. I'd slip out onto the balcony and watch as other doors slid open and shadowy figures stepped out. We were all listening to the surf (Will it be a rough swim today?) and thinking about the task at hand. Even though we were each relishing the last quiet moment in very personal ways, we were all doing it together.

• Treading water and waiting for 7:00, I notice the sun peeking from behind the stone church on Ali'i, its rays broken into fragments by the steeple. When I see that, I turn towards the Fairwind waiting for us at the turnaround. I know that it's only a matter of seconds before the cannon will sound, the butterflies in my stomach will disappear and I'll settle into the swim with the same thought that runs through my mind every year: "This is the moment I've been preparing for for the last 12 months."

• The moment that is surely one of the most emotional for me requires some back story. Most of today's Ironman courses are designed to be spectator-friendly, where the athlete sees crowds much of the day. Although some recent changes have kept the Kona bike course closer to spectators in the beginning, it's still a course where the racer spends many hours with no cheering crowds. As Julie Moss so aptly described racing here, "They send you out and hope you come home." The sun sets around 6:00 p.m., so for many age-groupers, the last part of the race will be in the dark, which makes for a very lonely and solitary experience.

Until the last turn at the Hot Corner onto Ali'i Drive. There, everything changes, and it happens fast. Where all was darkness, now it's brightly lit and filled with people and noise and celebration. As the finishing chute approaches, fatigue drains from the body and every racer feels like Joan Benoit must have felt in 1984 as she ran into the Olympic Stadium in Los Angeles to claim the gold medal.

But let's back up a few steps. For the first several years I did the race, just moments before that last turn onto Ali'i, during the final seconds of that quiet, painful solitude, there was a man standing calmly to the side away from the road, half-hidden in the dark recesses of some low trees. I never saw his face, but each year I heard his soft, gentle voice saying, *"Welcome home."* Each time I heard his simple two-word message, it brought a catch to my breathing and tears to my eyes. It was the first time since dawn that I let myself think about the enormity of the journey I'd been on all day and was about to complete.

One year he wasn't there. He hasn't been there since, and each time I pass that spot, I'm sorry that I didn't just once take a moment to find him and thank him.

- The final quarter mile down Ali'i is something you simply have to experience for yourself. Each of us who has been lucky enough to do it will remember it for a lifetime. The feeling is beyond description, but one thing is for sure: It's *better* than the hype.

- When I finally get into bed on race night, tired, sore and sunburned after covering 140.6 miles under my own power, I realize that, while I may have come back to the same place I started, I didn't come back the same person. Neither did any of the others among the 2000 of us who saw the sun break over the church steeple that morning. We all came back different. If you asked *how* we were different, you'd get 2000 different answers. And every one of them would be right.

- When I fly out, I look back on that thin, wind-blown road. The locals call it the Queen K. I call it the bike course. I say good-bye to my "playground" and silently promise myself I'll be back next October.

25 Kona People

Some runners follow their dreams; others hunt them down and beat them merciless into submission.
Neil Kendall

We all admire professional athletes. They seem to defy what we know of human limitations as they continue to set new records and higher standards. But the true inspiration, in my opinion, is the everyday athlete who puts it all on the line to test the limits of body and mind, without a sponsor to subsidize the effort. Driving this athlete is something very personal, maybe the opportunity of a lifetime to see what he's made of or a chance to set an example or maybe a special way of dealing with a life-threatening illness or the loss of a loved one. Whatever the reason, these folks work their training and racing around family, jobs and life's many demands to have their moment.

Back in my early days of racing Kona, there was a very devoted silver-haired couple who drew my attention because they raced every inch of the course together, and did it year after year. Katie Knight-Perry and her husband Ralph drew their strength and got their pleasure by making Ironman a duet. When they crossed the finish line, the accomplishment had been a joint effort and that was how they wanted their Ironman.

Katie Knight-Perry

Photo: Tim Carlson

One off-season I learned that Ralph had cancer. Shortly afterwards, he passed away. Several years later Katie came back to the Big Island and did the race solo. I saw her completing her day, running down Ali'i, alone in Kona for the first time, and I've never forgotten the look on her face. Those of us who saw her that night wondered where she summoned the courage to do that one last Ironman before hanging it up. I suspect it came from knowing that she wasn't truly alone and hadn't been all day.

Jim Howley was diagnosed with HIV in the mid-1980s. This was back in the days when that diagnosis was practically an automatic death sentence, so when it turned into full-blown AIDS, he was given 18 months to live. Jim, however, refused to believe it and fought back, big-time. Seven years after the diagnosis he stunned the medical community by completing the Ironman in Kona and a week later running the New York City Marathon. He went on to do more Ironman races, as well as the Transcontinental Triathlon for Life, where he ran, biked and swam 3,500 miles from Los Angeles to New York in 52 days. All these years later, he's still alive.

60-year old Babbette Kulka had tried for years to get into Kona. In 2001 the stars aligned and she got her ticket in but failed to make the bike cutoff. Two years later she got in again, and although she was the last competitor into T2, she made the cutoff. But around Mile 19 of the run, down in the Natural Energy Lab late at night where there is absolutely no light and a very rough, rutted road, she stepped wrong and hurt her ankle. It was a bad injury, one that should have forced her into the medical van heading back to the finish line. But this was her Kona experience and Babbette was not about to finish that way. She didn't make it back before midnight, the official cutoff, so was not considered an official finisher, but she made it back under her own power and finished on her own terms. In the hospital later that night she discovered that her ankle hadn't just been sprained...it was broken. Two months later she received a package from fellow competitor Robert Spina, who'd driven out onto the course that night and walked her to the finish line. Inside was Robert's finisher's medal, but with Babette's name engraved on the back.

There's the fellow whose bike seat broke, so he squished up a Gatorade bottle and sat on that. And the guy who was hit by a race scooter which destroyed his bike. He hadn't gone all the way to Kona to get knocked out of the race, so with six miles to go, he hefted his wrecked bike up on his shoulder, took off his biking shoes and *hiked* back to transition where he carried on with the marathon and, several hours later, crossed the finish line.

Christian Sadowski covering the last six miles of the bike leg

Kona finishers over the years have included a Catholic nun, a woman pronounced morbidly obese by her doctor, racers with missing limbs and racers with limbs that weren't functional, retired professional football and baseball players, actors and CEOs, mothers and fathers, sons and daughters — a whole spectrum of humanity. The list of finishers tells the story of where we live, how old

Sister Madonna Buder, the oldest female Ironman finisher. This was her 34th.

we are and what we do for a living. What that list won't tell is the story behind who we are and why we did it. But one thing is certain: We all have a story. We all wanted, for our own reasons, our big moment.

Aloha...and see you on the course!

Destiny does not do home visits. You have to go for it.
Carlos Ruiz Zafon

Photo: Bakke-Svensson/WT

Dick Hoyt and his son Rick, who has cerebral palsy, have toed the line at Kona together six times and finished twice, along with over two hundred other triathlons and sixty-five marathons.

Photo: Ironman

Iron seniors Max Burdick and Bill Bell raced Ironman right into their late 70s, Max with 9 finishes under his belt, Bill with 32

Jon Blais inspired us all by finishing the Ironman in 2005 five months after being diagnosed with ALS

ACKNOWLEDGEMENTS

No one ever does an Ironman without the support and encouragement of many others. So too with writing a book about Ironman.

I have met so many supportive and encouraging people in my Ironman journey – old and young, male and female, fast and slow, professional and amateur. Over the years you have offered your friendship, pushed me to be the best I can be and taught me everything I know about the sport. This book is the result and each of you has contributed greatly to it. I'm very grateful to you all.

Special thanks go to several folks who guided me through the writing process: David Minkoff of BioBuilde for his creative ideas on subject matter; Lisa Lynam who asked me to contribute to her wonderful book, *Triathlon for Women*; Bill Potts of WTC for his first read and helpful suggestions; Thomas Stengel and Hans Jürgen Meyer for their confidence in me as a writer.

Neither my Ironman experience nor this book would have been possible were it not for my husband, Lee. In 1991 he uttered the fateful words, "I think you should try this Ironman thing." From that beginning and every day since he's had undying faith in my ability to shine, sometimes when I myself was lacking in that faith. Whether I'm crossing the finish line first or sitting on the sidelines with an injury, he never lets me forget that I am, and will always be, part of a very special family. I am an Ironman.

He was the first to suggest I write a book. Nothing surprising about that...he believes I can do anything.

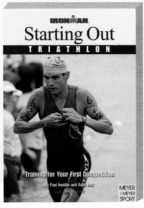

Starting Out

ISBN: 978-1-84126-101-0
$ 17.95 US / $ 25.95 CDN
£ 12.95 UK / € 16.95

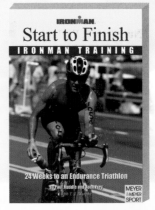

Start to Finish

ISBN: 978-1-84126-102-7
$ 17.95 US / $ 25.95 CDN
£ 12.95 UK / € 16.90

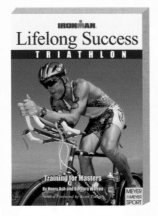

Lifelong Success

ISBN: 978-1-84126-103-4
$ 19.95 US/$ 29.95 CDN
£ 14.95 UK / € 18.90

Lifelong Training

ISBN: 978-1-84126-104-1
$ 19.95 US/$ 29.95 CDN
£ 14.95 UK / € 18.90

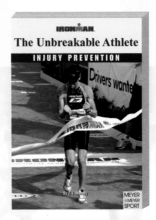

The Unbreakable Athlete

ISBN: 978-1-84126-109-6
$ 17.95 US/$ 25.95 CDN
£ 12.95 UK / € 16.90

Ironman Made Easy

ISBN: 978-1-84126-111-9
$ 16.95 US/$ 24.95 CDN
£ 12.95 UK / € 16.95

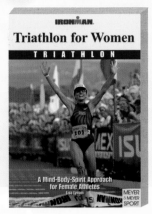

ISBN: 978-1-84126-105-8
$ 17.95 US/$ 25.95 CDN
£ 12.95 UK / € 16.90

ISBN: 978-1-84126-108-9
$ 16.95 US / $ 24.95 CDN
£ 12.95 UK / € 16.95

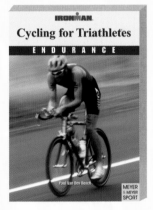

ISBN: 978-1-84126-107-2
$ 16.95 US/$ 24.95 CDN
£ 12.95 UK / € 16.95

ISBN 978-1-84126-112-6
$ 16.95 US / $ 24.95 CDN
£ 12.95 UK / € 16.95

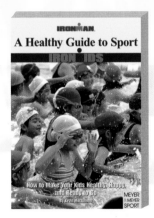

ISBN: 978-1-84126-106-5
$ 17.95 US/$ 25.95 CDN
£ 12.95 UK / € 16.90

ISBN: 978-1-84126-110-2
$ 16.95 US/$ 24.95 CDN
£ 12.95 UK / € 16.95

www.m-m-sports.com

MEYER
& MEYER
SPORT

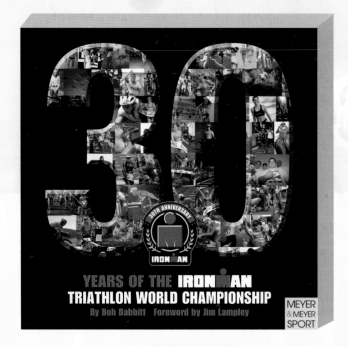

Bob Babbitt

**30 Years of the
Ironman Triathlon World Championship**

Ironman® Hall of Fame-Mitglied Bob Babbitt und einige
der weltbesten Sportfotografen beschreiben in diesem
Buch den Mythos einer Veranstaltung, die für viele den
ultimativen Härtetest im Sport darstellt: den Ironman®
Hawaii.

Mit vielen farbigen Fotos und spannenden Geschichten!

**Bildband
in englischer Sprache**
in Farbe, 200 Seiten,
geb., 25 x 25 cm,
ISBN 978-1-84126-114-0
$ 39.95 US / $ 44.95 CDN
£ 24.95 UK / € 29.95

MEYER
& MEYER
SPORT